Confirmation and Full Life in the Spirit

by Christopher Kiesling, O.P.

D0886169

Acknowledgments

Excerpts from the English translation of the Rite of Baptism for Children and the Provisional English translation of the Revised Order of Confirmation. Copyright © 1969, 1971, International Committee on English in the Liturgy, Inc. All rights reserved.

Excerpts from the New American Bible © 1970 used herein by permission of the Confraternity of Christian Doctrine, copyright owner.

Abbreviations

RC = the new *Rite of Confirmation*
RB = the new *Rite of Baptism for Children*

Revisores Ordinis
    Joseph E. Bidwill, O.P., S.T.Lr.
    Kevin D. O'Rourke, O.P., S.T.Lr., *J.C.D.*

Imprimi Potest
    Clement Collins, O.P., Provincial

Nihil Obstat
    Kevin D. O'Rourke, O.P., S.T.Lr., J.C.D.

Imprimatur
    ✠James J. Byrne, S.T.D.
    Archbishop of Dubuque
    January 17, 1973

S B N O-912228-09-1

To
my brothers in St. Dominic
in
the community of St. Rose of Lima
Dubuque, Iowa

Contents

Foreword

early in 1972 I was invited to give a talk on the sacrament of confirmation to the priests and religious educators of the diocese of Superior, Wisconsin. The talk was to launch a program of preparation for confirmation throughout the diocese. The letter of invitation informed me that the decision had been made to confer confirmation on adults in the spring of 1972 and on juniors and seniors in high school in the spring of 1973.

In the course of many years of teaching and writing about the liturgy and the sacraments, my thoughts about confirmation had begun to jell. I was inclined to think that confirmation should be reunited to baptism in one continuous rite, as it had been originally throughout the Church and still is in the Eastern Churches. But now I was being invited to talk to priests and catechists who would be preparing adults and junior and senior high school students for confirmation.

I would be of no help to these priests and religious educators if I told them that confirmation should be reunited to baptism and conferred on infants or that baptism should be deferred to later in life and conferred with confirmation. They had no power to make such changes. They had to deal with a given situation. On the other hand, I could not abandon certain convictions which I had formed about confirmation during several years of reflection. The only way of meeting this dilemma, I concluded, was to develop a theology of confirmation that was not dependent upon any particular age for the sacrament. This book is the result of the effort to meet that challenge.

No claim is made that this book presents *the* definitive theology of confirmation. Rather, it attempts to offer a theology of confirmation which will be helpful in the situation which prevails today in the United States. In our country currently, confirmation is conferred at just about every conceivable age, depending upon the diocese or the parish. A theology of confirmation which is bound inextricably to any particular age is obviously of value only to those people who live and work in a diocese or parish which confers confirmation at that age.

The theology of confirmation offered here may appear to run counter to the ideas which liturgical scholars are proposing about the integrity of the rite of Christian initiation, that is, the sequence of baptism, confirmation and the eucharist. The intent of this book, however, is not to argue against the proposals of liturgical scholars. But until their proposals can be adopted, there is need for a theology which makes sense out of prevailing practices. The purpose of this book is to present such a limited theology.

This book, moreover, does not profess to present all the theology of confirmation. Its purpose is to make sense out of what is going on in regard to confirmation.

To make sense, it is not necessary to say everything that could be said. Hence neither the conservatively inclined person nor the liberally inclined should construe my not mentioning some traditional idea about confirmation as a denial.

I wish to thank Reverend Harold Dodge, director of the Office of Religious Education of the Diocese of Superior, for the invitation to speak to the priests and religious educators of that diocese and for the inspiration which led to this book. I am grateful to Frances Voss and to my Dominican colleagues, Joseph E. Bidwill, Thomas McGonigle, Kevin D. O'Rourke, for their reading the manuscript and offering suggestions. I alone, of course, am to be held responsible for the final product. Thanks is given also to Ursula Neyens, my secretary, who typed the several manuscripts through which this book evolved. Finally, I am grateful for the encouraging enthusiasm of Reverend Jeremy Harrington, O.F.M., the editor of St. Anthony Messenger Press, the publisher of this book.

—Christopher Kiesling, O.P.

Dubuque, Iowa
January 28, 1973

Chapter One

A Puzzling Sacrament

archbishop Fulton J. Sheen made news in February, 1967, when he announced a program of religious education for the Diocese of Rochester, New York. This program would result, within a few years, in the conferral of confirmation on young people at the age of 17 or 18, rather than the age of 10 or 12. The bishop was breaking with the familiar custom in the United States of confirming children in grade school. That custom is still, by far, the predominant one. But today more dioceses are delaying confirmation to later in life, or are adopting late confirmation as one of several options, or are studying the question of the appropriate age for confirmation. Confirmation is a puzzling sacrament today partially because Church legislation, actual practice, our liturgical heritage and pastoral concern offer different answers to the question of when the sacrament should be conferred.

Time for Confirmation

According to canon 787 of the Code of Canon Law, in the Latin Church confirmation may be deferred to around the age of seven, although it may be conferred earlier in danger of death or for some other serious reason. The new *Rite of Confirmation* (n. 11) repeats the norm that confirmation is generally postponed until about the seventh year, but allows for territorial conferences of bishops to choose a more appropriate later age. "Deferring" and "postponing" imply that some reasons exist for confirmation earlier than around seven years of age. These reasons are the baptism of infants and the nature of confirmation as the complement of baptism. If a child is baptized, the nature of confirmation, as traditionally understood, dictates that it be conferred on the child soon afterwards. In the Eastern Churches it follows immediately upon baptism. In dioceses of Spain and Latin America it is conferred a couple of years later, before seven years of age.

Actual practice in this country only approximates observance of the law. The period of time around the seventh year is consumed in preparing children for first communion and also for the sacrament of penance before first communion. There is no time to prepare them also for confirmation. Besides, the bishop's availability in a large diocese is limited. So confirmation is delayed until later years in grade school.

The sequence of sacraments actually followed in this country is baptism, penance, eucharist and confirmation. Hence actual practice violates our liturgical heritage. In that heritage baptism and confirmation lead to the eucharist. The three sacraments constitute the "rites of initiation" into the Church. Penance follows incorporation into the Church insofar as there arises a need for reconciliation to the community into which one has been initiated. This sequence of the sacraments in the ancient

6

Church is still followed in Eastern Churches. It is possible in the Western Church when the candidate for baptism is old enough to be catechized; then he or she is to be baptized, confirmed and given the eucharist (RC, n. 11). The new liturgy of the Roman rite stresses the unity of the rites of Christian initiation, but actual directives leave enough openings for contrary practices.

Pastoral concern urges even later confirmation than is now prevalent. It offers this answer, different from that of legislation, current practice and our liturgical heritage, because it believes that later confirmation would slow down the rise of the number of people who are Christians in name only. Too many people go by the name of Christian or follow merely the externals of Christian life because they were baptized as infants, received the eucharist around the age of seven and, shortly afterwards, were confirmed while still children. But the values by which they actually live are those of secular society, not those of Jesus Christ. Later confirmation would promote more mature, serious commitments to Christian life.

Soldier of Christ

Confirmation is a puzzling sacrament, secondly, because of different views of what it is and what it does. For a long time confirmation was said to make the baptized Christian a soldier of Christ. It equipped a person for spiritual combat against the forces of evil. The bishop's tap on the cheek after the anointing with chrism was interpreted as a symbol of the attacks of evil which the candidate would henceforth have to resist.

This idea of confirmation gained prominence in the Middle Ages. It was attributed to a fourth century pope,

7

Melchiades, in a letter among a set of forged documents called the *False Decretals*, compiled in the ninth century to enhance the authority of bishops. Pope Melchiades never existed. The idea was actually expressed toward the end of the sixth century by Faustus of Riga, a minor bishop of southern Gaul, today France. These facts have become known only in recent times. The idea carried great weight with medieval theologians, however, because they thought it was the idea of a pope. Hence the idea became a central notion in the explanation of confirmation.

The idea is not entirely without merit. The view that confirmation "arms" the Christian for combat is very old; it is found as early as the late second and early third centuries in the writings of Tertullian. Confirmation, moreover, has always been related to Christian witness, which the Apostles gave with courage after the Holy Spirit descended upon them at Pentecost. Combating evil and bearing witness to Christ can be considered two sides of the same coin. Finally, "confirmation" does mean "strengthening."

But this view of confirmation has its deficiencies. Its origin deprives it of the privilege of being *the* understanding of the sacrament, even though it contains some truth. Baptism, moreover, introduces one to spiritual combat, as is indicated by the dramatic rite of rejecting Satan and professing Trinitarian faith in the baptismal celebration. Ignatius of Antioch recognized this aspect of baptism in the early second century. Furthermore, this idea is not supported by the tap on the cheek given by the bishop. Rather than a symbol of the attacks of evil, the tap on the cheek is a sign of affection, a form of the kiss of peace; it expresses the bond of love between the bishop

8

and the members of his flock. In addition, the idea of a soldier of Christ is too militaristic to be appealing in our day. The concern for peace in our day finds the image of soldier unsuitable for describing the Christian who is called by Christ to be a peacemaker, not a warrior (Matt. 5:9). Finally, scholars generally agree that, whatever its merits, the idea does not get to the heart of confirmation.

Gift of the Holy Spirit

Closer to the truth is the idea that confirmation bestows the Holy Spirit. In the present Roman rite of the sacrament, the words accompanying the anointing with chrism and the prayers surrounding this central action indicate the belief that in confirmation God bestows on the candidate the Holy Spirit. The same idea emerges from the rites of confirmation found throughout the history of the Church, both in the East and in the West. Popular preaching and teaching about confirmation throughout history also express this understanding.

But there are difficulties with this idea, at least in so simple a form. Both the rites of baptism and confirmation indicate that the Holy Spirit is conferred in baptism. The theology of baptism as incorporation into Christ and the fruits of his victory over sin and death requires that the gift of the Holy Spirit be included among the blessings of baptism. The theology of grace also requires the Spirit to be given in baptism, for baptism bestows so-called sanctifying grace which entails the indwelling of the Spirit. No one, moreover, can be saved unless he is quickened by the Holy Spirit. The baptized but unconfirmed can be saved; confirmation has not been considered absolutely necessary for salvation, though it is helpful in achieving the fullness of Christian life.

The idea that confirmation confers the Holy Spirit cannot be saved simply by saying that, although baptism confers the Holy Spirit, confirmation bestows more of him. The Holy Spirit is not a thing to be parceled out in pieces. He is a personal, spiritual being. His influence may increase in our lives and hence his presence may be more prominent, but he himself does not increase.

To say that confirmation confers a new presence of the Holy Spirit over and above the presence effected through baptism raises the question of just what this new presence is. Some more or less evident basis must be given for affirming a new presence of the Holy Spirit through confirmation. It does not seem likely that this basis is some change in him but in us. What, then, is this change in us? This idea of confirmation needs development in order to be a satisfactory explanation of this sacrament.

That development may take the direction of affirming that confirmation intensifies the influence of the Holy Spirit in our lives. Because of confirmation, we follow Christ more closely; we are more vigorously and thoroughly inspired by his Spirit. But this effect can hardly be distinctive of confirmation since the eucharist exists precisely to nourish life in the Spirit of Christ.

Finally, confirmation may be regarded as giving the Spirit in the sense of protecting or guaranteeing the gift of the Spirit given in baptism. Confirmation "seals" the blessings of baptism. Like the ideas of increased presence of the Spirit and intensified life in the Spirit, this idea contains some truth. But like them, it is not adequate. The eucharist serves to sustain and so protect the gift of the Spirit bestowed in baptism. Moreover, some Christians persevere and even advance remarkably in the life of the Spirit without confirmation.

Sacrament of Commitment

A popular idea today is that confirmation sacramentalizes commitment to Christ or ratification of baptism. This idea lies behind the trend to delay confirmation to later years in high school or even into adulthood.

No quarrel can be had with the desire to foster more mature commitment to Christ, but there are difficulties in saying that confirmation is the sacrament of commitment or ratification of baptism. The rites of confirmation and the Catholic understanding of these rites throughout the centuries offer little evidence that confirmation's essence, even in part, is personal commitment or baptismal ratification. Confirmation does not "elevate" personal commitment to a sacramental status, as the sacrament of penance elevates sorrow for sin or as the sacrament of matrimony elevates the exchange of marriage vows. Confirmation may be an occasion or even a cause of baptismal ratification or Christian commitment, but to call it the sacrament of ratification or commitment is not accurate. Moreover, this idea of confirmation results more from the wish to meet the needs of Christian life in contemporary secular society than from an understanding of the sacrament's inner nature. The needs are real enough, but that confirmation is meant to handle them is not so obvious.

Sacrament of Maturity

Another popular idea is that confirmation sacramentalizes entrance into adulthood. Societies generally have rites of passage from childhood to adulthood. The transition between these two stages of life involves dramatic changes. The young become physically capable of begetting and bearing children. New powers of intelligence develop. New responsibilities loom in the future. All these novelties generate fears, guilt, and shame, even as they inspire desire, hope, and enthusiasm, so that this period is one of emotional turmoil. This transition period is mysterious and bewildering to those going through it. It is important to society, for out of it must come those who will ensure the society's continuation. Primitive peoples respond to it religiously, as a time of contact with the sacred, the holy, the origin of all things. Their religious response takes concrete form in religious rites of passage.

Even sophisticated secularized cultures have their rites of passage. Some are organized, like graduations from grade school, high school and college. Some are not organized, except insofar as they become the "in" thing for young people to do. These informal rites of passage may involve pranks, defiant behavior, vandalism and other antics which annoy adults but which are meant to prove to the young person and to society that he or she is no longer a child but a self-reliant adult.

In the Christian religion, as this line of thought would say, confirmation is the rite of passage from Christian childhood to Christian maturity or adulthood. It is appropriately celebrated at the beginning of adolescence to help the young person through that period of life, or toward the end of that period to mark the attainment of maturity approaching adulthood.

The weakness of this view of confirmation is the danger of conveying a distorted idea of Christianity and of confirmation by confusing faith and religion. Religion is man's relationship to God arising out of man's needs experienced in personal and social life. For example, life is filled with change and uncertainty. Not only does man grow through stages of life, but the world around him changes, sometimes very suddenly, unexpectedly, violently. He feels insecure. His knowledge and mastery of himself and the world are limited. He encounters personal and social problems which alone and even with others he cannot solve. He feels powerless. To cope with his insecurity and powerlessness, he turns to the eternal, all-knowing, omnipotent and provident Creator and Lord of the universe.

Faith, on the other hand, is man's relationship to God arising out of God's revelation to man. Religion is response to man's need; faith is response to God's word. Man's need is the measure of religion; God's revelation is the measure of faith. Christianity is, first of all, faith, a response to God's revelation in Jesus Christ. The religious element which Christianity contains is subordinate to the faith element. Christian faith in response to God's word controls man's religious response to the needs which he experiences.

The New Testament, the basic witness to God's revelation in Jesus Christ, pays no special attention to the stages of human life and the transition between them. It contains no evidence that Jesus had a special message for teenagers, a special program tailored to those difficult years or a special ritual to mark the beginning or end of that phase of life. Faith, which controls the religious elements in Christianity, neither requires nor forbids religious rites of passage.

To present confirmation as a sacrament of maturity comparable to the religious rites of passage for adolescents in other societies, religious or secular, risks conveying the idea that Christianity is just religion, or just another religion. It opens the door to the notion that Christianity is simply a God-oriented satisfaction of human needs rather than an invitation to become "sharers of the divine nature" (2 Pet. 1:4), that is, to participate in a life which fulfills human needs but, at the same time and more importantly, transcends all human exigencies. Such distorted thinking about Christianity would very likely entail misconceptions of confirmation. Its character as a form of the word of God addressing and calling us to a radical conversion from human standards to the reign of God could be obscured. Its significance for the whole of one's life and not just a phase of it could be missed. Its efficacy for the whole community could be overlooked.

Akin to Ordination

An appealing idea of confirmation understands it as the sacrament for the Church ministries performed by lay men and women (including religious sisters and brothers), as ordination is the sacrament for Church ministries performed by clergymen. We speak of "Church ministries" and not simply "Christian ministries." In fulfillment of their baptismal vocation to bring Christ's message and love to all men and women, Christians render services on their own initiative and in their own names, and people recognize them as acting on their own. These services are Christian ministries. But the baptized may also render services precisely as representatives of the Christian community and in its name, and are recognized by the public as so doing. These services are Church ministries.

14

Bishops, priests, and deacons obviously exemplify those performing Church ministries. But lay people (including religious) also can and should perform Church ministries. Their Church ministries do not appear to be blessed by a sacrament, however, as the Church ministries of the clergy are. But, the argument proceeds, reflection on confirmation reveals that it is the sacrament for Church ministries of lay people. This fact has been obscured by the conferral of confirmation on everybody, usually at an early age and without any clear explanation and demonstration of its connection with Church ministry by the laity. Now we are more conscious of the Church as the whole people of God, and we appreciate the role of the laity in the life and mission of the Church. So we can put confirmation in its proper place and use it for its proper purpose, that is, as the sacrament conferring upon lay people a ministry in the name of the Church.

But one wonders if such an interpretation of confirmation is not more than a discovery of the true nature of the sacrament. In the light of the traditional use and understanding of confirmation, this idea appears to assign a radically new nature to confirmation. The sacrament is narrowed down from a celebration of the Holy Spirit in and for Christian life generally to a celebration of the Holy Spirit as enabling a particular activity, namely, lay ministry in the name of the Church. In pulling confirmation away from baptism and relating it to ordination, this notion not only goes against the long-standing practice and conception of confirmation as a sacrament of initiation; it also calls for a profound change in the theological understanding of the relations of grace and the so-called sacramental character involved in the sacrament.

16

Acceptance of this idea of confirmation would imply a willingness to admit that the Church can abandon a sacrament and initiate a new one.

Rite of Initiation

We have just mentioned the familiar idea of confirmation as a sacrament of initiation. This idea is ancient and has endured through many centuries into the present day in the larger Christian Churches. Not only has the idea endured, but even the practice has continued to a very great extent. Where the practice has lapsed, current teaching and legislation endeavor to restore it. A wealth of liturgical scholarship insists upon this conception of confirmation.

Nevertheless, there are difficulties with this notion of confirmation. It does not fit the facts of life. In many places, in spite of what is taught about the sacrament, it is received after other sacraments, notably penance and the eucharist. Sometimes it is received after one has lived an exemplary Christian life for many years. Some remarkable witnesses to Christ have never been confirmed, while a host of confirmed Christians are mediocre disciples of Christ.

Into what does confirmation initiate a person? It does not simply incorporate one into the mystery of Christ or into the Church, for baptism accomplishes these initiations. To say confirmation initiates one "more fully" into either the mystery of Christ or into the Church is not very enlightening. Confirmation as initiation into the Pentecostal mystery, in contrast to baptism as initiation into the Easter mystery, is a beautiful thought; but it is difficult to see what this means in terms of everyday Christian life.

17

Baptism incorporates a person into Christ's priesthood, prophetic office, and royal messianic reign, as both the theology of baptism and its rite attest. Hence, confirmation does not appear to be distinguishable simply as initiation into one or another or some combination of these prerogatives of Christ. Baptized people are called to bear witness to Christ and actually do so. So confirmation is not distinguished as initiation into Christian witness. To say that confirmation constitutes a baptized person, not simply a son or daughter of God, but a son or daughter "in power," is not very illuminating. These and many other ways of distinguishing confirmation from baptism as rites of initiation are not entirely satisfying.

The Charismatic Movement

Puzzlement over confirmation has been increased in the past dozen years by the charismatic or Neo-Pentecostal movement in the Roman Catholic Church and other main line Churches. This movement stresses the work of the Holy Spirit in Christian life. In particular, it puts great value on the various marvelous gifts which the Spirit inspires in people for building up the body of Christ. These gifts, it claims, are not extraordinary phenomena meant only for the first Christians in order to draw attention to the newly-born Church in a Jewish or pagan world. These gifts are for all ages of the Church and are integral to the ordinary life of the Christian community. St. Paul gives a generous sampling of these gifts in his first letter to the Corinthians:

To each person the manifestation of the Spirit is given for the common good. To one the Spirit gives wisdom in discourse, to another the power to express knowledge. Through the Spirit one receives faith; by the same Spirit another is given the gift of healing, and still another receives miraculous powers. Prophecy is given to one; to another power to distinguish one spirit from another. One receives the gift of tongues, another that of interpreting the tongues. But it is one and the same Spirit who produces all these gifts, distributing them to each as he wills (I Cor. 12:7-11).

The New Testament Greek word for gift is *charisma;* hence the name "charismatic" for the movement stressing these and similar gifts. A number of Christian sects throughout history, and especially since the beginning of the 20th century, have made the manifestation of the Holy Spirit through these charisms or gifts their central doctrine. They are known as Pentecostal denominations. Among the more prominent in the United States are the Assemblies of God, the Pentecostal Holiness Church, the International Church of the Foursquare Gospel, the Pentecostal Church of America, the Pentecostal Assemblies of the World, and the United Pentecostal Church. Because the charismatic movement in the main traditional Churches shares some of the Pentecostals' ideas, it is sometimes called the Neo-Pentecostal movement.

The charismatic movement puts great stock in what is called "baptism of the Spirit." This is a personal experience of the Holy Spirit's presence and of his taking over the direction of one's life. This personal experience is very often accompanied by some manifestation of the Spirit's presence, such as speaking in tongues (that is, some unintelligible language), or interpretation of these strange utterances or healing through prayer and perhaps the laying on of hands. Even if such charisms are not present, many Pentecostals hold, baptism of the Spirit is a profound experience which results in a notable change in one's vision and values. It produces a conversion in one's life.

Perhaps the most remarkable fact of the past decade is that — whatever name is given to it — many Catholics and other Christians have experienced such conversions. Mediocre Christians have become zealous. Christians alienated from the institutional Church, its liturgy and its programs, have become faithful members of a charismatic group. They spend hours in its prayer sessions and enthusiastically share with others their newly-discovered joy in the Holy Spirit. The richness of their new life often enables them to find fresh significance in the institutional Church, its worship and its mission.

This movement is a source of puzzlement about confirmation because charismatics appear to have the experience of the Holy Spirit and to manifest his presence in their lives in a way we would expect of the confirmed. Confirmation is supposedly the sacrament which, in some sense, bestows the Holy Spirit and his gifts. Yet after a confirmation ceremony we rarely hear the newly confirmed testifying to a profound interior experience of the indwelling Spirit, and still more rarely do we witness them speaking in tongues, interpreting them, prophesying, healing or manifesting other marvelous gifts of the Spirit. Instead, we find these phenomena occurring in those who were confirmed many years previously and who afterwards often lived mediocre Christian lives. We also find them occurring in people who were never confirmed.

20

These facts challenge the Church's doctrine that confirmation is the sacrament of the Holy Spirit. Also, the high value placed by the charismatic movement on baptism of the Spirit tends to put in question the value of the sacrament of baptism by water in the name of the Trinity. What is the relation of baptism of the Spirit to the sacraments of baptism and confirmation?

Protestant Interpretations

The diversity of notions about confirmation is increased if we take into account Protestant views. Within Protestantism, many different ideas about confirmation have been proposed in the course of history and are proposed today. To state a general Protestant view is very difficult because Protestant ideas of confirmation vary so much from denomination to denomination.

Protestant understanding of confirmation, insofar as it is influenced by the great reformers Martin Luther and John Calvin, does not recognize confirmation as a sacrament. It is simply a rite developed by the Church, not instituted by the Lord. It is, however, an important rite of the Church. It is considered as a ritual for personal ratification of one's baptism received in infancy; or it marks the completion of, or an important moment in, Christian catechesis or education; or it admits a person to full membership in the Church, or a Church, with the privileges and duties such membership entails. Until most recently, the major Protestant Churches have insisted that confirmation precede communion in the Lord's Supper. This practice is now being questioned and even changed.

Many Protestant Churches are wrestling as much as the Roman Catholic Church with the theology and practice of confirmation. Protestant and Catholic theologians sometimes arrive at very similar interpretations of confirmation. An important Protestant contribution in this rethinking of confirmation is insistence on the primacy, dignity and perfection of baptism. The theology and practice of confirmation should not belittle baptism.

Mystery

The multitude of practices and theories in regard to confirmation can bewilder us and lead us to despair of making sense of the sacrament. But this variety can also lead us to some valuable positive affirmations about confirmation. The first of these is that it is a mystery in the sense that we describe life as a mystery.

When we say this, we do not mean that we do not and cannot know life. On the contrary, we know it very well; we live it, experience it, recall it, anticipate it and can affirm with the utmost certainty that it is. But for all our familiarity with it, we never understand it thoroughly or master it completely. The folklore and literature of many cultures and nations from ancient times to the present strive to express the meaning of life and to explore its twists and turns. Yet we cannot find one story, one drama, one novel or a collection of them which does more than throw light on one or several facets of life, leaving much more of it in the shadows. The human sciences — anthropology, psychology, sociology — provide vast amounts of information and numerous theories about life; but in so doing, they only emphasize that actual life is a marvelously rich reality in which we share intimately and deeply, which we know, but which continues to baffle intelligence and elude control.

Christian life, that is, human life inspired by the

Spirit of Jesus Christ, is also a mystery. We experience it and know it when we experience and know faith, hope, love, joy, peace, patience, kindness and generosity in a community of men and women or in individuals or in ourselves. Our experience and knowledge of disbelief, despair, hatred and other opposite qualities only intensify our wonder at the life in the Spirit which we do encounter. Yet the dogmas and doctrines of Churches and the theologies of scholars, which express some understanding of life in the Spirit, do not put an end to all questions about it or provide a blueprint for its development in any individual. Life in the Spirit of Christ is as much an adventure into the known unknown as the human life which it enriches.

Confirmation is one of the many acts or moments that constitute Christian life. It shares the mysterious quality of that life. The Christian community and its members experience and know confirmation as in some way celebrating the Holy Spirit in their lives. They confer confirmation now at one age, now at another, not so much as the result of deliberate choice but because many factors in the flow of life in a particular era and place favor one age over another. Confirmation is explained now in this way and now in that. But however Christians handle it or explain it, the reality of it escapes comprehension; it remains a mystery. The vagaries of practice and the diverse interpretations of confirmation are not the result of its poverty of meaning and power but, on the contrary, flow from its richness. Its full reality escapes our understanding and control, so that we have difficulty in saying definitively that it is this or that, does this or that, belongs here or there in a lifetime.

In our effort to make sense of confirmation, a first

step is to recognize that it is a mystery. To acknowledge this is not to avoid the problems which the sacrament poses for us. We are not saying that it is impossible to understand confirmation. We are saying that our understanding begins by acknowledging that we are dealing with an element in the mystery of Christ-in-us (cf. Col. 1:27). This mystery is a gift which God, not man, dispenses and controls. It is a gift so rich that, though experienced and known, it is never so well understood or used that there are no more questions about it.

A Religious Expression

A second affirmation about confirmation concerns the rite of the Church which embodies it. That rite must be regarded as principally a religious expression and not a theological statement. It expresses Christians' knowledge and experience, in faith, of the fact of the Holy Spirit in their lives. Confirmation is a moment in Christian life when consciousness of the Spirit in that life is heightened through prayers and the symbolic gesture of a bishop's anointing candidates with chrism. The purpose of this heightened awareness is to renew faith in the Holy Spirit and to foster openness to his influence. Its purpose is not to answer questions about the nature of the Holy Spirit, the compatibility of his influence with human freedom or the appropriate age for the sacrament. Answering such questions is the business of theology and pastoral care, not of sacramental rites. Rites are a part of the religious mystery about which theology asks and answers questions.

Official Church teaching about confirmation must also be regarded as predominantly on the level of religious expression rather than on the level of theological

statement, although theology influences this religious expresssion. With this understanding we must read what has been said by the Church in councils (especially Florence and Vatican II) about confirmation. The same understanding must be applied to the Introduction to the rite of confirmation in the *Roman Pontifical* (the book containing ceremonies in which bishops preside) and the statement of Pope Paul VI announcing the new rite of confirmation (an apostolic constitution entitled *Divinae Consortium Naturae*).

These official statements of the Church tend to bring together affirmations about confirmation which have their origins at different times in the course of history when critical knowledge of history and the Bible were not so greatly developed as they are today. Some of these affirmations do not fit together very well among themselves. Some appear irrelevant today. Some conflict with the findings of critical historical research into the past, the results of scholarly exegesis of the New Testament, the carefully reasoned conclusions of theology and the pastoral programs suggested by psychological and sociological research.

But the official pronouncements of the Church, though influenced by scholarship and theology, are first of all and primarily expressions of Christian consciousness of the mystery of Christ, statements of faith and of experience in faith. They point people in the right direction so that they can enter into the mystery of Christ. These statements are not concerned about removing all the problems which critical history, biblical exegesis, theological explanation and pastoral skill raise. They are concerned about introducing people into the mystery of Christ in all its fullness.

The religious nature of the rite of confirmation and official Church teaching about confirmation means that, in our effort to make sense of confirmation, we have to interpret the rite and official statements. We cannot simply report the rite and collect official declarations because they make no pretense to answer all the questions we have.

We wish to keep in mind, above all else, that our questions aim to make sense of a living religious reality which the rite expresses and is part of, which the Church's official teaching points toward and which we experience and know obscurely but surely in faith, hope and love. That mysterious religious reality — the actual celebration of confirmation in the Christian community for some of its members — is what we are trying to understand.

Chapter Two

A Sacrament of Initiation

I was walking along Canal Street, just across the Chicago River outside downtown Chicago's Loop, toward the Northwestern Railroad station. From Monday to Friday this street is filled with trucks, cabs and cars. In the early morning and late afternoon, thousands of commuters stream across it on their way to and from work in the mass of towering buildings across the river. The air is filled with the rumble of traffic and the fumes of engine exhaust. But at 10:30 on this mid-summer Saturday morning, Canal Street shared the ghostly bleakness which descends upon the commercial district of any major city on weekends. The street was empty and the sidewalks unpeopled. The buildings lining the street were storehouses of palpable emptiness and their closed windows were blind, staring eyes. Silence weighed heavily on the street. The atmosphere was still stale from the week's traffic.

A lone car appeared, coming toward me down the street. It was light blue, old and battered. A woman was sitting very close to the man driving. Behind the car a few tin cans on a rope clattered on the pavement. As I turned my head to watch the car pass, I saw the cardboard and crayon sign tied on the back: "Just married." The car went its way down the deserted street and I continued in the opposite direction toward the railroad station.

I thought of the couple in the car. I wondered where they were going and if they were to meet friends for a dinner and singing and dancing and laughter. I suspected not. The celebration of their marriage would probably not extend very far beyond those tin cans clattering behind their car on desolate Canal Street. So desperate and pathetic a celebration of so momentous an event!

A Need to Celebrate

Yet it was a celebration. This lonely couple had to tell themselves and the world that an important event had occurred in their lives. Something had happened to them to which they and others had to pay attention. They knew on that Saturday morning joy, hope, fears and apprehensions, which they had to express in order to share them with others and to win others' support.

Celebration is an ingredient of human life. Animals do not celebrate the anniversaries of their herd's origin or of individuals' birthdays. Celebration is not, of course, a materially useful activity; it does not directly increase the Gross National Product. Nevertheless, it is a humanly useful activity; it yields human products. It heightens consciousness and knowledge of persons, institutions, events and their values. It generates feelings about these things and consequently influences decisions in regard to them. It also influences people's interaction; it binds them together and separates them from others; it pro-

30

vides mutual support. Through celebration one generation communicates to another its awareness and knowledge, feelings and decisions, actions and interactions.

Celebration is even necessary in order to be human. To be human requires awareness of self, life, others, the world. It demands emotional responses to these, decisions about them and interactions with them. Through symbolic words, actions, things, personages and images celebration brings these human characteristics into existence, sustains them and intensifies them.

Because it is necessary for human life, celebration permeates life, but it takes many different forms. It may be elaborate, like a banquet with speeches, or simple, like informal conversation with a friend over a cup of coffee. It may be a major celebration marking an important event, like the inauguration of the President of the United States; or it may be minor, like a phone call to tell a neighbor about a bargain purchase. A wedding is a joyful celebration, while a funeral is sorrowful. Formal celebration is found in a graduation ceremony and informal celebration in an "open house" on Sunday afternoon. The presentation of Oscar awards is an explicit celebration and a students' "bash" after exams an implicit one. A bridal shower is a planned celebration, but a drink with an old friend after a chance meeting is spontaneous. Celebration may be public, like a Fourth of July parade, or private, like a couple's having dinner together on their wedding anniversary.

Any actual celebration, of course, combines several of these features; and varieties of combination result in the many different celebrations woven into the tapestry of life. But whatever its form, celebration heightens consciousness of some factors in life worthy of understanding and response, conditions feelings about those factors, influences decisions about them and so develops personal growth and relations to others and the world.

The Sign of the Spirit

An obviously significant event in a person's life is God's sending his own Holy Spirit into his or her life. By that gift of the Spirit the person is freed from sin or estrangement from God and ultimately even from death. He or she begins a life which fulfills human aspirations beyond comprehension. God's gift of his Spirit for a life of love, joy, peace, patient endurance, kindness, generosity, faith, mildness and chastity (Gal. 5:22-23) may come with a mature person's faith in Jesus Christ as the sign and source of that gift of the Spirit. God, who wants all men to be saved and come to know the truth (I Tim. 2:4), may send his Spirit into the life of a child or infant in answer to the prayer of those who already are inspired and guided by his Spirit and who desire their offspring to enjoy the same inspiration and guidance. God also sends his Spirit into the lives of men and women who, although not believers in Jesus Christ, live as uprightly as they can in response to their consciences and sincerely seek God in and beyond the many manifestations of him in creation, history, personal life and the religions of the world.

The gift of life in the Holy Spirit is ordinarily given to, and lived out by, individuals in community. We receive our humanity, our talents, our culture, education and profession from the human community which precedes us and surrounds us. There is room for individual initiative and creativity in our personal lives; we are not determined completely by society. But we do get our start from society and work out our personal development in relation to other men and women in a variety of communities. The same holds true for Christian life.

The Father and the risen Lord communicate their Spirit to men and women through the Christian community. The people of God are animated by the one Spirit whom the Father and the Son send into the hearts of its members. Through their ministry, the Father and the risen Jesus communicate their Spirit to other men and women. Thus the Christian community is the sacrament of the Spirit of God, that is, the sign or witness of the Holy Spirit given to men and women, and the instrument which the Father and Christ employ to communicate their Spirit to other men and women.

The Father and Christ, however, are not limited to the Christian community for the manifestation or the communication of their Spirit. So no one should be surprised to find non-Christian men and women sharing the attitudes of Jesus and doing deeds similar to his. But through the Christian community those attitudes and deeds are explicitly recognized and nourished as Christlike, as participation in Christ's paschal mystery and as the gift of the Holy Spirit.

Celebrating a Changed Life

The sending and reception of God's Spirit into one's life merits celebration. That gift means a radical change in life, from being ensnared in a basically good but morally crippled humanity, to being caught up in God's redemptive action operative in the world and proclaimed especially (we Christians believe) by the community of believers in Christ risen from the dead. All that is implied in this gift of God and change of life should be brought clearly into the consciousness of those to whom

God gives his Spirit so that their lives may be directed in accord with what the Spirit would accomplish in them. The values inherent in this gift and new life should be displayed so that feelings may respond to them and decisions be made in pursuit of them. The support of others should be gained to help in living by the Spirit.

This heightened awareness, display of values and lending of support are achieved in the Christian community's liturgical gatherings. There the Christian people hear the word of God and seek to understand what it has to say about life in the Spirit whom God has given them and they have received. In praise and thanksgiving they reflect on God's marvelous gift of the Spirit revealed in the history of salvation and Jesus Christ. They pray for that gift to be continuously given to the community and individual members. They declare in word and gesture that God through Christ does indeed grant his Spirit in view of Christ's assurance that whatever his disciples ask in his name will be given to them.

The gift and reception of the Spirit not only merit celebration but in actuality have been celebrated for centuries by the Christian community. In so doing, the community has been following the natural human need and propensity to celebrate various experiences of life in order to live them humanly (that is, conscious of them, and affectively and freely responding to them) and to communicate them from one generation to the next.

Baptism

Jesus provided the celebration for the gift of the Spirit whom the Father gave to him and offers to all men. His own baptism in the Jordan, when the presence of the Spirit in him was manifested, was an obvious model for his disciples' celebration of the gift of the same Spirit. Jesus also described his disciples as those who take up their cross and follow in his footsteps (Mark 8:34; Matt. 16:24; Luke 9:23). Luke 12:50 attributes to Jesus a reference to his death on the cross as a baptism which he ardently desired. The undertaking of Christian discipleship quite naturally, then, was expressed in baptism. Jesus' disciples understood baptism, in the likeness of Jesus' own baptism in the Jordan, to be an apt celebration of participation in Jesus' death and resurrection which the gift of the Spirit of Jesus makes possible. Moreover, the words ascribed to Jesus, "No one can enter into God's kingdom without being begotten of water and Spirit" (John 3:5), suggest that the first Christians understood it to be Jesus' wish, even command (Matt. 28:19), that the new life of faith in him engendered by his Spirit be celebrated by baptism.

In the Acts of the Apostles we find evidence that the first Christians celebrated new life in the Spirit of Christ by baptism. The first converts to the gospel preached by Peter on Pentecost Sunday did not merely give mental assent to his message. Their repentance of their past was not only an interior sorrow. Nor was the trust they placed in Jesus as their savior limited to the depths of their hearts. They did not merely secretly welcome the gift of his Spirit. They also demonstrated or celebrated through the rite of baptism what God was doing in them and what they were doing in response (Acts 2:37-38, 41). St. Paul, in the sixth and eighth chapters of his letter to the Romans, explains in great detail the meaning and consequences of the baptismal celebration. He shows what factors in Christian life that celebration brings into heightened consciousness, what feelings and decisions it promotes, what support it provides for the following of Christ.

Even when the Spirit of Christ had obviously already been received by the centurion Cornelius and his relatives and close friends, the Spirit's coming into their lives was celebrated by baptism. Peter had not finished speaking of Christ to Cornelius and his companions *when the Holy Spirit descended upon all who were listening to Peter's message. The circumcised believers who had accompanied Peter were surprised that the gift of the Holy Spirit should have been poured out on the Gentiles also, whom they could hear speaking in tongues and glorifying God. Peter put the question at that point, "What can stop these people who have received the Holy Spirit, even as we have, from being baptized with water?" So he gave orders that they be baptized in the name of Jesus Christ* (Acts 10:44-47).

Another manner of celebrating the gift of the Holy Spirit, also recorded in the Acts of the Apostles, was prayer and the imposition of hands. Many Samaritans, hearing the preaching of the good news by Philip the deacon, believed in Jesus and accepted baptism.

When the apostles in Jerusalem heard that Samaria had accepted the word of God, they sent Peter and John to them. The two went down to these people and prayed that they might receive the Holy Spirit. It had not as yet come down upon any of them since they had only been baptized in the name of the Lord Jesus. The pair upon arriving imposed hands on them and they received the Holy Spirit (Acts 8:14-17).

At Ephesus St. Paul found some disciples who had

been baptized with the baptism of John and who claimed that they had not even heard of the Holy Spirit. Paul then explained John's baptism to them as a preparation for Jesus' coming. "When they heard this, they were baptized in the name of the Lord Jesus. As Paul laid his hands on them, the Holy Spirit came down on them and they began to speak in tongues and to utter prophecies" (Acts 19:5-6).

This second way of celebrating the gift of the Spirit by prayer and the imposition of hands has been interpreted in the past as the sacrament of confirmation. Both the Samaritans and the Ephesians had been baptized before prayer was said over them and hands laid on them. Moreover, the rite of confirmation, at least in the Western Church, has involved prayer for the coming of the Holy Spirit and the imposition of hands in some fashion.

Biblical scholars today, however, are very reluctant to identify the apostles' imposition of hands in these two cases as confirmation. Although the imposition of hands has been involved in the Church's rite of confirmation, that gesture has been less prominent than anointing with oil. Moreover, confirmation has not usually been accompanied by unusual phenomena such as occurred in these two instances (see Acts 8:18-19;19:6). The gift of the Spirit associated with confirmation has also been regarded as more basic to Christian life than the gift of the Spirit enabling a person to speak in tongues, prophesy or perform other marvelous deeds.

Biblical scholars see some other celebration in these impositions of hands. One good possibility for the Samaritan episode is that the apostles' laying on of hands celebrated the fact that the Spirit comes through the ministry of the Church, represented by the college of the Twelve in Jerusalem. Another possibility is that the imposition of hands celebrated the conferral of a Spirit-inspired ministry to bear special witness to Christ through prophecy and speaking in tongues. The imposition of hands in the Ephesian episode may also have been a celebration of an unusual ministry; or it may have been simply a gesture spontaneously added to the act of baptizing to bring out the fact that baptism and its benefits are conferred through the ministry of the apostolic Church.

Tracing the History of Confirmation

We have to admit that we know very little about confirmation in the earliest days of the Church and for many decades afterwards. However, we have evidence, from the latter part of the second century, that the Christian community had developed an elaborate celebration of the gift and reception of life in the Spirit of Christ. To the simple ceremony of baptism in water in the name of Jesus or of the Trinity, the Church had added other symbolic gestures and prayers.

Such development may have begun in apostolic times if the opinion is correct that Paul's imposition of hands upon the Ephesians was simply part of their baptism. There might be an allusion to such development in the reference to the imposition of hands in Hebrews 6:2, which refers to "instruction about baptisms and laying-on of hands." This instruction would be aimed at distinguishing Christian baptism from Jewish baptism of converts, the baptism of John and the water purifications of the Qumran community, a kind of monastic Jewish sect from whom came the famous Dead Sea Scrolls. The

39

laying-on of hands, about which there was also instruction, refers probably to the conferral of some Church ministry or mission (as in Acts 6:6, 13:3; I Tim. 4:14; 5:22; II Tim. 1:6) or to that gesture as a sign of an extraordinary coming of the Spirit, as in the case of the Samaritans and Ephesians.

Whenever the development began, there is evidence in the writings of St. Justin Martyr, from the middle of the second century, that considerable ceremony had developed around the simple act of water baptism. We are informed by Tertullian in his works *On Baptism* and *On the Resurrection of the Flesh,* dating from around the juncture of the second and third centuries, that Christian initiation included not only washing with water (baptism) but also an anointing with oil, signing with the cross and the imposition of the bishop's hand. Writing shortly after Tertullian, St. Cyprian indicates that the Christian initiation ceremonies embraced not only baptism in water, but also the imposition of the bishop's hand and a signing with the cross of the Lord.

The Apostolic Tradition, written by St. Hippolytus in Rome about 215, gives the first detailed picture of the Church's celebration of the gift and reception of life in the Spirit of Christ. Scholars agree that the celebration which Hippolytus reports must have been in vogue since at least the end of the second century, for he professes to report traditional practices. Since confirmation as distinct from baptism developed out of rites of Christian initiation such as Hippolytus describes, it is helpful to review what he reports.

Baptism was preceded by a three-year catechumenate or period of instruction. The catechumens were regularly instructed, prayed together apart from the faithful and were dismissed with a blessing and the imposition of hands by the teacher. When catechumens drew near to the time for their baptism, they were set aside as the "elect" or the "competent." On Holy Thursday they bathed, and on Friday and Saturday they fasted. On Saturday the bishop assembled them and again prayed over them, laying his hand on them, that they be freed from evil.

Saturday night was spent in vigil, hearing the Scriptures read and being further instructed. Toward the morning of Easter Sunday, prayer was said over the baptismal water. Then the catechumens renounced Satan and were anointed by presbyters (priests) with the Oil of Exorcism. A presbyter then baptized the candidates, who went naked down into the water with a deacon, or with a deaconess in the case of women.

The presbyter asked the catechumen if he believed in the Father. After he responded, "I believe," the presbyter, having his hand upon the candidate's head, immersed him once in the water. This procedure was repeated twice again as faith was professed in Christ Jesus and in the Holy Spirit. Parents or someone from the family spoke for children who could not speak for themselves. The candidates then emerged from the baptismal water and were anointed with the Oil of Thanksgiving by the presbyters; in the case of women, presbyters anointed only the head; deaconesses anointed the rest of the body.

Having put on their clothes, the newly baptized went from the baptistry to the assembly of Christians in the church. There the bishop laid his hand upon them and prayed for the gift of the Holy Spirit for them. The bishop then poured consecrated oil into his hand and laid his hand on the head of each candidate, saying: "I anoint you with holy oil in God the Father Almighty and Christ Jesus and the Holy Spirit." The bishop then "sealed" the candidate by making the sign of the cross on his forehead. After giving him a kiss of peace, the bishop said, "The Lord be with you," to which the candidate answered, "And also with you."

Then prayers were said — the Prayer of the Faithful. The Eucharist followed. Besides the consecrated bread and wine, the newly baptized also received milk and honey, symbols of the Promised Land.

Evidence exists for similar celebrations of initiation from various parts of the world during the third and subsequent centuries, for example, St. Cyril of Jerusalem's catechetical instructions and St. Ambrose of Milan's explanation of the Christian mysteries, as the sacraments were called in Greek and early Latin. Naturally variations are found from place to place and from time to time. But a general pattern prevailed in the rites of Christian initiation.

The part of the celebration preceding the Eucharist was called "baptism" or "the seal" (*sphragis* in Greek). Only in the fifth century did a distinct name, "confirmation," appear for that part of the initiation celebration which included the bishop's invocation of the Holy Spirit, imposition of his hand, anointing with oil and signing with the cross.

Besides acquiring a distinctive name, the postbaptismal rites ascribed to the bishop became separated from baptism in the western part of Christendom. In the course of the fourth and fifth centuries, the Church, with the freedom and patronage it attained under Constantine, began to spread much more widely into rural areas from the cities where it had initially been established throughout the Roman Empire. Now all prospective new members of the Church could not be gathered in the bishop's see city for Christian initiation.

In the East, this problem was solved by bishops' allowing presbyters (priests) to invoke the Holy Spirit and anoint the newly baptized with chrism consecrated by the bishops on Holy Thursday. This practice still prevails in the East. In the West, the problem was solved by omitting from Christian initiation those rites carried out by the bishop and deferring them to a later time when the bishop would come from the see city into the outlying districts to "complete" the baptism. This practice is still typical in the West, although the Eastern solution is possible in certain circumstances.

The separation of the confirmation rite from the baptismal rite and the eucharist led ultimately to heightened consciousness of confirmation as a distinct sacrament. This consciousness expressed itself clearly and definitively, however, only in the High Middle Ages with the development of theological reflection on the sacraments. Unfortunately, this separation also led to an exaggerated distinction of confirmation from baptism, an overly-inflated importance attached to confirmation and a breakup of the dynamic unity of the rites of Christian initiation: baptism, confirmation and the eucharist.

Christ's Institution of Confirmation

In this evolution of the distinct rite which became known as the sacrament of confirmation, we can see

why some thinkers at the beginning of theological speculation in the Middle Ages attributed the institution of confirmation to the Apostles rather than to Christ. We can see why the 16th-century reformers could deny its being a sacrament at all and affirm that it is merely an important rite instituted by the Church for one or another purpose.

Catholic theologians for a long time proceeded to show that Jesus did explicitly establish confirmation as a sacrament, even as he did baptism and the eucharist. Sometimes they appealed to tradition as handing this bit of information on, even though the New Testament does not mention it. Sometimes they gathered from the Scripture what we might call circumstantial evidence of Christ's institution of confirmation. Allusions to confirmation are found in the prophecies of an outpouring of Yahweh's Spirit: Isaiah 44:3 and Joel 3:1-2 (2:28-29 in some versions), the latter being quoted by Peter in his discourse on Pentecost Sunday (Acts 2:16-18). The New Testament records Christ's promise of the Holy Spirit (John 7:38-39; 14:16-17, 26; 15:26; 16:7-14). It records the apostles imposing hands on the Samaritans and Ephesians after baptism and their receiving the Holy Spirit. Hebrews 6:2 refers to baptisms and the laying on of hands. From all this evidence, viewed especially in the light of tradition, it was argued that even Scripture testifies to Christ's having instituted the sacrament of confirmation, although the testimony is not as clear-cut as in the cases of baptism and the eucharist.

In recent decades, however, Catholic theologians have largely abandoned this approach to Christ's institution of confirmation and other sacraments. A basic reason for taking a different approach is recently acquired understanding that the four Gospels are not histories of Jesus' life like modern biographies of famous men. They are witnesses to the early Christian community's faith in Jesus. They contain interpretations of Jesus' words and actions. These interpretations arose in the process of using Jesus' words and actions to solve problems of Christian life which arose in the community. The Gospels do contain historical facts, but the Gospels' objective is not to report all the words and deeds of Jesus in the exact order of their occurrence and in precisely the form and circumstances in which they were spoken or done, as we expect of contemporary biographies. In a similar way the Acts of the Apostles is not simply a lengthy newspaper-like account of the development of the early Christian community. It includes an interpretation of facts.

In the light of this understanding of the Gospels and the Acts of the Apostles — an understanding shared by many Protestants — is it difficult even to say that the New Testament reports actual explicit commands of Jesus to celebrate baptism and the eucharist, although such commands are attributed to Jesus by the biblical authors (Matt. 28:19; Mark 16:15-16 for baptism; Luke 22:19; I Cor. 11:24-25 for the eucharist). Much less readily then can we point to certain chapters and verses of Scripture as reports of Christ's institution of confirmation or other sacraments.

What has just been said should not be interpreted to mean that Jesus did not express his will that there be the various sacraments. Although all the words put in the mouth of Jesus in the New Testament may (note: *may*) not be verbatim reports of his speech, they do express what the first disciples of Jesus understood him to be saying to them in his words and actions. They express God's revelation through Jesus in its reception by the disciples. From the New Testament witness we can rightly conclude that Jesus did promise the Holy Spirit to those who believed him and followed him, that he wished them to live in mutual love and service according to the Spirit and that he wished his followers to carry to others his message of the coming kingdom of God. In this sense, at least, he willed a missionary community animated by his Spirit; he founded a Church.

He also indicated some of the ways in which this missionary community should live together, nourish its bond with him and bear witness to him. For example, even if (note *if*) Jesus did not explicitly command on some specific occasion that baptism should inaugurate membership in the community of his followers, he provided by his own baptism in the Jordan a model for the undertaking of Christian discipleship. By celebrating a religious meal with his disciples on the eve of his passion and death, by giving a new meaning to that meal and by eating with his disciples after his resurrection, he provided his followers with a way of regularly celebrating their life in his Spirit. Neither Jesus nor his disciples as Semites would have thought it possible to have a missionary community animated by the Spirit which did not express its faith, hope and love externally in ritual activity. Unlike ourselves, they had not inherited a dualistic notion of man as a soul imprisoned in the body (Plato) or a mind inhabiting a machine (Descartes). So the biblical authors had good reason to attribute to Jesus explicit commands to celebrate life in his Spirit by the symbolic rites of baptism and the eucharist.

The mission of the Spirit-filled community founded by Jesus is to bring to men and women God's justifying, reconciling, sanctifying grace or favor revealed in Jesus' message and especially in his own death and resurrection. In the course of its history, the Christian community has discerned in its many activities certain ones which, in a supreme, exemplary, paradigmatic way, express and convey to men and women God's redeeming love for them.

God's love is expressed and conveyed by the community itself as a community of love in the likeness of God's and Christ's own love. The community itself is sacramental, a sign and bearer of God's gracious love; the Church is the fundamental sacrament (cf. Vatican Council II, *Constitution on the Church,* n. 1; *Constitution on the Liturgy,* nn. 1, 26; *Constitution on the Church in the Modern World,* n. 45). All of its activities in some way express and convey God's favor reconciling men and women to himself and to one another. But certain of these activities stand out: the preaching of the Word and what are known as the seven sacraments. It was obvious from the beginning that the preaching of the Word expressed and conveyed God's love to men and women. From the beginning also it was clear that God's love was manifestly bestowed in baptism and the eucharist. In the course of time the Christian community discerned that surely his loving kindness is expressed and granted in other activities.

When the Christian community celebrates with a sinner his repentance and welcomes him back to the community's life and to God, surely God's gracious redeeming love is expressed and conveyed in that celebration. Thus the sacrament of penance was recognized as a return to one's baptismal vocation. A crucial time in the life of a baptized person is sickness unto death from illness or old age. Then he or she is called to suffer unto death in the likeness of Christ, not merely symbolically and interiorly, as in baptism, but actually and exteriorly in bearing bodily suffering. Certainly when the Christian community prays over the sick or the old and expresses to God its care for them by anointing them, God hears this prayer and shows his gracious help to those liable to death. If God were not to help men and women at such a moment through his Church, one wonders why there should be a Church at all. If the Church exists for anything, it must exist to help men suffer unto death in Christ. Thus the sacrament of the anointing of the sick supplements baptism to help men live out to the end their baptismal vocation.

Surely God's gracious help is offered to those who are called by God and by the Christian community to assume primary public responsibility for the ongoing life of the community. So ordination to the episcopacy, priesthood, and diaconate (divisions of the office of primary public responsibility for the community) was recognized as celebrating God's gracious enabling love, that is, as being a sacrament. If God's gracious love accompanies the baptized person throughout his or her life in order that he or she may live as a true disciple of the Lord, surely that gracious help continues to be given to them in their marriage to one another. But now it is God's grace to live Christian life as "two in one flesh," a particular way of living Christian life with its own unique witness to Christ's love for mankind, different from the way and

49

witness of Christian life as a single person.

God's gracious love is undoubtedly bestowed on men and women in and through other activities of the Christian community and of individual Christians. For example, the community's acceptance of profession to follow Christ in poverty, celibacy and obedience is certainly a grace-filled event. Reconciliation between friends who have fallen out with each other is also a grace-filled event. Assuming responsibility for the welfare of one's family or some portion of the human family is not without the offer of God's gracious aid. Thus the Christian community can recognize many activities which express and bear God's grace to men and women. But the Christian community has chosen, under the influence of Jesus' own teaching and work as understood and recorded in the New Testament, to recognize seven paradigmatic activities, along with the preaching of the Word, as instances of God's grace coming to men and women through the ministry of the Church and its members. These paradigmatic or model instances of God's bestowal of grace through the ministry of the Church have become known as the seven sacraments.

Because these activities have been chosen in the light of Jesus' own teaching and work as understood and recorded in the New Testament, it is possible to find Scriptural bases for them in at least some general and prophetic way. We may not be able to cite a chapter and verse as indisputable evidence for Christ's institution of each of them, but we can find bases to help us see that they are in accord with God's and Jesus' intention in giving birth to a missionary community to bring the gracious love of their Spirit to men. Hence, the older approach of theologians to Christ's institution of the seven sacraments is not entirely void of value and meaning.

Christ's institution of several of the sacraments implied in his providing a missionary community to carry on his redemptive work applies to confirmation. More specifically, we may say that Christ's institution of confirmation is implied in his provision of a community which would celebrate entrance into Christian discipleship by baptism. The sacrament of confirmation is implied in the sacrament of baptism. Baptism celebrates God's gift of Christ's Spirit who makes possible belief in Jesus, taking up one's cross and following him. But as a celebration of this gift and reception of the Spirit, baptism heightens consciousness especially of the call and possibility to take up the cross and follow Jesus in death and resurrection. As we saw in the evolution of the Christian rites of initiation, the simple ceremony of baptism was expanded by additional ceremonies which more obviously celebrated the gift of the Spirit: first the imposition of hands and then later anointing with chrism, both with prayer calling upon God to send his Spirit to the baptized.

Thus baptism and confirmation are celebrations of the same event — the gift of the Spirit for following Christ in death and resurrection; but each celebrates more emphatically diverse elements or aspects of that event. In the first centuries of Christianity, the two celebrations were woven together with the eucharist in one continuous celebration of Christian initiation, but in the Western Church the continuous celebration was broken up, so that confirmation emerged as a distinct sacrament or, better, a distinct sacramental act, complementing baptism.

So some Catholic theologians today speak of

Christ's instituting confirmation directly or immediately, that is, he himself willed it. He did not institute it indirectly or mediately, that is, through authority which he gave to the Church to institute sacraments. But Christ's direct or immediate institution was not necessarily explicit, that is, couched in some clear, precise command about confirming disciples. It was, rather, more or less implicit in his provision for the continuance of his redemptive work through a community which, in carrying out this work, would inevitably see in its celebration of the gift of the Spirit the efficacious visible sign or sacrament of that gift.

If Protestants do not acknowledge confirmation as a sacrament, that denial may be largely the result of their decision to call a "sacrament" only those celebrations which Scripture explicitly attributes to a command of Christ. Although Protestants may not call confirmation a sacrament, they may still regard it in practice as a celebration of the gift of the Spirit in some sense. If Catholics and Protestants were to look at the realities of their lives rather than the language they use to describe them, they might find themselves in greater agreement than they are generally aware of.

Confirmation as Initiation

The sacrament of confirmation emerged clearly into Christian awareness only gradually over the centuries. It came into the light in the process of the Christian community's development of the rites of initiation. Because confirmation was recognized in this process of developing the rites of initiation, it became known as a sacrament of initiation, along with baptism and the eucharist.

But in many areas of the Western Church including

the United States, confirmation is no longer a sacrament of initiation in the original sense. It no longer introduces a person to the eucharist, the full life of the Christian community, and the other sacraments. Instead, the eucharist precedes confirmation and — a still more violent disruption — penance precedes the eucharist.

If we are going to make sense of confirmation as a sacrament of initiation, we have to have another interpretation of "sacrament of initiation." The phrase cannot be understood to refer to a sacrament which is conferred before the eucharist and the other sacraments. "Sacrament of initiation" must be understood theologically rather than chronologically and ritually. It may be desirable to be able to interpret the phrase in all three ways. But we cannot do so now, given the present, deeply rooted custom of deferring confirmation and the tendency to postpone it to still later in life. We probably will not be able to do so for some time to come. However, it may also be desirable, for pastoral reasons, to be content with only a theological interpretation of "sacrament of initiation."

A sacrament of initiation may be defined theologically as a sacrament which celebrates those components, aspects and developments of life in the Spirit of Christ which are always present and operative, at least implicitly, in all circumstances of life. In contrast, the other sacraments celebrate those components, aspects, and developments of life in the Spirit of Christ which are present and operative in special circumstances of life. A glance at the various sacraments will clarify this definition of a sacrament of initiation.

All the sacraments may be seen as concerned with the same thing: the gift of abundant life in the Holy

Spirit in the likeness of Christ in his death and resurrection. The sacraments differ from one another by bringing into heightened consciousness different elements, aspects and developments of this life and different influences which the Spirit would have in the lives of men and women, thus enabling them to follow Christ more closely in all the circumstances of their lives.

Some components, aspects and developments of life in the Spirit are always actually present and operative, at least subconsciously or implicitly. Without them, there would be no Christian life. Life in the Spirit always implies, for example, faith in Jesus Christ, love of God and of neighbor, self-sacrifice, following the lead of the Holy Spirit, rejection of sin, continuous resistance against the forces of evil within and without, worship of God and witness to his grace and message in Jesus Christ. The sacraments of initiation — baptism, confirmation and the eucharist — bring into heightened consciousness these perpetually necessary factors of life in the Spirit so that, by the power of the Spirit, men and women can shape their lives in the likeness of Christ. How these three sacraments of initiation differ from one another will be explained in Chapter 4.

Some elements, aspects and developments of life in the Spirit come into play only in certain circumstances. Life in the Spirit involves repentance and renewed reconciliation with God only insofar as, after baptism, one still succumbs to sin. It involves bearing grave physical suffering, and the weakness of the human spirit which such suffering entails, only when one is afflicted with suffering unto death in serious illness or the debility of old age. It involves faithful conjugal love and care for children only when a person is married. It involves selfless dedication to the Christian community when one is ordained to the office of primary public responsibility for the welfare of the community. These factors of life in the Spirit are brought into heightened consciousness by the sacraments of penance, anointing of the sick, matrimony and ordination so that followers of Christ may, by the power and guidance of the Spirit, put on Christ in these special situations.

Although confirmation today in the United States is usually not a sacrament of initiation chronologically and ritually, it is one theologically. Though it may be received late in one's life, after the reception of other sacraments, it nevertheless celebrates initial, that is, basic or fundamental, components, aspects and developments of Christian life generally. Precisely what these basic factors are will become evident in the chapters which follow.

Chapter Three

The Holy Spirit's Fullness in Us

"**i**f I had only known then what I know now, how differently I would have acted!" Most of us have probably thought this way one or more times in the course of our lives. We did not study for a coming biology examination because we thought we knew the answers. After doing poorly in the exam, we realized how much there is to be known about the living cell. Or we let contact with a good friend die, realizing only much later how rare a good friend is and how fine a friend we lost. Anyone looking back over a career or a marriage recalls instances when he would have acted differently if, at the time, he had the knowledge of the business or of his partner which he now has years afterwards. We may be satisfied with the choices which we have made and would not have the courses of our lives be different than they were. Still how much more joy we would have derived from those choices if we had known how right and good they would prove to be in the end.

We might look back over our lives as Christians and say, "If I had only known then what I know now! If I had only realized years ago how rich my life could have been because of my Christian faith! I've not known the deep peace, the quiet self-confidence, the sustaining inspiration that other Christians have found in the experience of God's acceptance and in deep prayer. I've not felt the unique carefreeness of those who have spent themselves more for others' happiness than for their own. Though I have regarded myself as a Christian, I have been careful not to let it be too obvious; I wonder how many people I have failed because I feared to give them a word of Christ.''

The sacrament of confirmation is meant to help Christians never to have to say of their Christian lives, "If only I had known!" The gift of life in the Spirit of Christ is first celebrated in baptism. To help the baptized make the most of that life, the Christian community has confirmation.

In confirmation the Church celebrates the richness and potentialities of life in the Spirit. It celebrates the profoundly satisfying and wonderfully uplifting elements in Christian life: sensitivity to God's presence in our lives; filial love of God flowing into generous love of neighbor; insight into the meaning for us of God's revelation in Jesus Christ; perception of the value of people, institutions, and events in our lives; ability to see each of life's moments in relation to God's coming kingdom; discernment of the truly human and Christian thing to do in baffling situations; and courage in adversity. It celebrates Christian life's potentialities whereby we "will be able to grasp fully, with all the holy ones, the breadth and length and height and depth of Christ's love, and experience this love which surpasses all knowledge, so that [we] may attain to the fullness of God himself" (Eph. 3:18-19). It celebrates the potentialities whereby we "may be found rich in the harvest of justice which Jesus Christ has ripened in [us], to the glory and praise of God" (Phil. 1:11).

The richness and potentialities of Christian life celebrated in confirmation derive from the Holy Spirit. Dwelling within us, he helps us with his infinite power and guides us with his infinite wisdom, so that, if we go along with him, our lives are rich and potent for even greater richness. Hence we may say that the sacrament of confirmation celebrates the richness and potentialities of Christian life as the Holy Spirit's fullness-in-us. The aptness of this designation of the mystery which confirmation celebrates will become clear first by noting an obvious fact about confirmation, then by qualifying this fact in the light of Scripture and the rite of baptism and, finally, by examining the revised rite of confirmation itself.

The Rite of Celebration

Confirmation obviously celebrates the gift of the Holy Spirit in some sense. The rite of confirmation is clear. After the renewal of baptismal vows by the candidates, the bishop invites the people to pray, saying:

> *My dear friends:*
> *By baptism God our Father gave these adopted children*
> *new birth to eternal life.*
> *Let us ask him*
> *to pour out the Holy Spirit upon them,*
> *to strengthen them in their faith,*
> *and anoint them to be more like Christ the Son of God.*

A pause for silent prayer follows. Then the bishop and the priests assisting him impose their hands over all the candidates, the bishop alone saying:

> *All powerful God, the Father of our Lord Jesus Christ,*
> *by water and the Holy Spirit*
> *you freed these candidates from sin.*
> *Send your Holy Spirit upon them*
> *to be their Helper and Guide.*
> *Give them the spirit of wisdom and understanding,*
> *the spirit of right judgment and courage,*
> *the spirit of knowledge and love,*
> *the spirit of reverence in your service.*
> *[We ask this] through Christ our Lord.*
> R. *Amen.*

Then the bishop moistens his right thumb with chrism and makes the sign of the cross on the forehead of each of the candidates. As he does so, he says:

> *N., receive the seal of the Holy Spirit, the Gift of the Father.*

The newly-confirmed answers:

> *Amen.*

The bishop then gives the candidate some sign of peace.

Modification from Scripture

In the light of Scripture we must qualify the bestowal of the Holy Spirit referred to in this rite of confirmation. According to Scripture the Holy Spirit is given in bap-

61

tism. When the crowds asked what they must do in response to Peter's preaching on Pentecost Sunday, he answered: "You must reform and be baptized, each one of you, in the name of Jesus Christ, that your sins may be forgiven; then you will receive the gift of the Holy Spirit" (Acts 2:38).

In St. Paul's thought, the Holy Spirit is given in baptism. By baptism into Christ, we are clothed with Christ; by faith in Christ, of which baptism is the expression, each of us becomes a son of God (Gal. 3:26-27). The evidence of this sonship acquired through faith expressed in baptism is the fact that "God has sent forth into our hearts the Spirit of his Son which cries out 'Abba!' ('Father!')" (Gal. 4:6).

"Through baptism into his [Christ's] death," St. Paul writes, "we were buried with him, so that, just as Christ was raised from the dead by the glory of the Father, we too might live a new life . . . dead to sin but alive for God in Christ Jesus" (Rom. 6:4, 11). Being alive for God in Christ Jesus entails the Holy Spirit's dwelling within us:

You are not in the flesh; you are in the spirit, since the Spirit of God dwells in you. If anyone does not have the Spirit of Christ, he does not belong to Christ. If Christ is in you the body is dead because of sin, while the spirit lives because of justice. If the Spirit of him who raised Jesus from the dead dwells in you, then he who raised Christ from the dead will bring your own mortal bodies to life also, through his Spirit dwelling in you (Rom. 8:9-11).

Referring obviously to baptism, Paul writes to the Corinthians that "you have been washed, consecrated, justified in the name of the Lord Jesus Christ and in the

Spirit of our God" (1 Cor. 6:11). He then urges the Corinthians not to defile through sin their bodies which have become the temple of the Holy Spirit: "Do you not see that your bodies are members of Christ? . . . You must know that your body is a temple of the Holy Spirit, who is within — the Spirit you have received from God" (1 Cor. 6:15, 19).

According to many, perhaps most authorities, Paul is alluding to baptism when he writes to the Corinthians: "God is the one who firmly established us along with you in Christ; it is he who anointed us and has sealed us, thereby depositing the first payment, the Spirit, in our hearts" (2 Cor. 1:21-22); and again when he writes to the Ephesians: "You were sealed with the Holy Spirit who had been promised. He is the pledge of our inheritance, the first payment against the full redemption of a people God has made his own, to praise his glory" (Eph. 1:13-14). The Holy Spirit is given to us at baptism as a kind of down payment on the wealth of blessings that will eventually be ours.

More evidence could be adduced from the New Testament to show that the Holy Spirit is given in baptism to be an interior source of life in Christ. No definitively convincing arguments have been offered to support the supposition that the word "baptism" in the New Testament generally refers to a complex rite which included, besides washing in water, an imposition of hands or an anointing. In other terms, the word baptism in the New Testament does not include another rite, later known as confirmation, which, rather than baptism in water, conferred the Holy Spirit. The conferral of the Spirit through the laying on of hands in Acts 8:14-19 (by Peter and John on the Samaritans baptized by Philip the deacon) and Acts 19:1-7 (by Paul on the Ephesians after their baptism in the name of Jesus) must be interpreted, as we did in Chapter 2, in a way which respects the over-all teaching that the Spirit is given in baptism by water.

Qualification from the Rite of Baptism

The bestowal of the Holy Spirit referred to in the rite of confirmation must be understood also in the light of the rite of baptism. The rite of baptism expresses the Church's belief that the Holy Spirit is bestowed in that rite. In a prayer in the style of an exorcism begging God to free the baptismal candidates from the forces of evil (*Rite of Baptism for Children*, n. 49) the minister of the sacrament prays:

> *We pray for these children:*
> *set them free from original sin,*
> *make them temples of your glory,*
> *and send your Holy Spirit to dwell with them.*

There is no hint that the sending of the Spirit to dwell within is expected to be answered in the distant future in some rite other than the baptism which will shortly take place.

In the blessing and invocation of God over the baptismal water (RB, n. 54), the celebrant says:

> *In the waters of the Jordan your Son was baptized by John and anointed with the Spirit.*

Jesus' being "anointed with the Spirit" is a metaphor for his being filled and inspired by the Spirit as the Messiah (the Anointed-one) and as the Suffering Servant of Yahweh, who would save mankind by his death and resurrection. That Jesus was so anointed by the Holy Spirit was strikingly manifested at his baptism in the Jordan (Matt. 3:16-17; Mark 1:9-11; Luke 3:21-22). The baptismal rite's reference to Jesus' own baptism by water and his anointing by the Spirit implies that the candidate's own baptism in water in imitation of Jesus' will entail receiving the Holy Spirit.

After the baptism itself, the newly-baptized is anointed with chrism (RB, n. 62). The meaning of this anointing is announced by the minister:

> God the Father of our Lord Jesus Christ has freed you from sin, given you a new birth by water and the Holy Spirit, and welcomed you into his holy people. He now anoints you with the chrism of salvation. As Christ was anointed Priest, Prophet, and King, so may you always live as members of his body, sharing everlasting life.

Now Jesus is priest, prophet and king par excellence because he has been anointed by the Holy Spirit in the most profound way. If the post-baptismal anointing signifies that the baptized person, as a member of Christ's body, becomes a participant in Christ's threefold dignity, then it signifies the baptized person's reception of the Holy Spirit.

The question may be asked, however, if this gift of the Spirit conferring a share in Christ's triple role is not a distinct event from the gift of the Spirit giving new life in baptism by water. The announcement before the anointing suggests this idea.

In answer it may be noted that water-baptism alone bestows upon a person all the blessings of Christ risen from the dead. Through Christian life and the other sacraments a person enters more fully into those blessings; they penetrate more deeply into his life, shaping it in the likeness of Christ. But the blessings are not parceled out one after the other. So this anointing with chrism after baptism in water is not symbolic of another distinct gift of the Spirit beyond that of the water-baptism. Rather, this anointing bears explicit witness to certain aspects of the single but many-faceted event celebrated by the baptismal washing.

Moreover, in the prayer for the consecration of chrism on Holy Thursday, the bishop says:

> *By this sacrament [of chrism]*
> *give them [those who are to be born again in the*
> *waters of baptism] the fullness of royal, priestly,*
> *and prophetic honor,*
> *and clothe them with the robe of unending life.*

Here the gift of the threefold honor is tied up with "clothing with the robe of unending life." This "clothing" occurs in baptism. Furthermore, the gift of unending life is mentioned after that of sharing in Christ's triple dignity. This order is very odd if the share in Christ's mission as priest, prophet, and king is a distinct gift conferred after water-baptism in a separate rite, either the post-baptismal anointing or the sacrament of confirmation. On the other hand, if the gift of the Holy Spirit and participation in Christ's three roles are only different aspects of one event, it makes no great difference which is mentioned first.

Finally, the baptismal rite contains several references to new birth, rebirth and new life "by water and the Holy Spirit" (RB, nn. 53, 54, 56, 62, 70, 219, 224, 247). This phrase, "by water and the Holy Spirit," is not to be interpreted to mean that the Holy Spirit remains, as it were, "outside" of the baptized person, from afar influencing his life in some way through the medium of water. It means, rather, that when the person is washed in water, the Spirit, in virtue of that person's faith or the faith of the Christian community, enters into his life to dwell within him and inspire his activities. The coming of the Spirit into the inner man to help and guide him is the counterpart of the external washing in water. The baptismal rite provides two pieces of evidence for this understanding.

In one of the alternate sets (RB, n. 219) of the General Intercessions (the Prayer of the Faithful), there is the petition:

> *Once they are born again of water and the Holy Spirit, may they always live in that Spirit, and make their new life known to their fellow men.*

If the Spirit is not given in baptism, it would be impossible for the baptized person to "*always* live in that Spirit."

In one form of the blessing and invocation of God over the baptismal water (RB, n. 224), the celebrant praises God:

> *You have set us free and filled our hearts with the Spirit of your love, that we may live in your peace.*

If the Spirit does not actually "fill our hearts" when we are washed in the baptismal water over which this praise is offered, the prayer leads us to expect from being washed in that water an event which will not happen. The prayer is then misleading.

Of course, new birth and new life "by water and the Holy Spirit" must be interpreted in the light of Jesus' baptism, which Christian baptism imitates. In Jesus' baptism, as we have noted, the Spirit was manifested as coming down upon him to be an effective force in his life (Luke 3:21-22, 4:1, 14).

The Spirit's Fullness

From the data of Scripture and the baptismal rite recounted here, as well as from other data that could be brought forward from Scripture and theology, it is clear that the gift of the Holy Spirit celebrated in confirmation must be qualified. A hint as to what this qualification might be is found in the sample invitation to prayer at the conclusion of the baptismal rite. The invitation says that "in confirmation they [the newly baptized] will receive the fullness of God's Spirit" (RB, n. 68).

This expression, "the fullness of God's Spirit," makes sense if confirmation reflects the abundant outpouring of the Holy Spirit on Pentecost. Confirmation's mirroring the Pentecostal event is suggested by the sample homily of the new *Rite of Confirmation* (n. 22), by the fourth question which the bishop puts to the confirmation candidates in the renewal of their baptismal promises (RC, n. 23), and, less explicitly, by the third part of the bishop's concluding blessing (RC, 33A). Linking confirmation to the mystery of Pentecost, moreover, is common in theology. It plays an important role, for example, in Edward Schillebeeckx's theology of the sacraments in his *Christ the Sacrament of the Encounter with God*.

But the "fullness of God's Spirit" cannot mean that quantitatively more of the Holy Spirit is given in confirmation. The Holy Spirit is not a quantitative thing which can be doled out in pieces. He is a spiritual and personal being. Nor can the fullness of the Holy Spirit conferred in confirmation be an intensification of his own being, powers or activity for his own perfection. The Spirit is God, already the plenitude of being, power and action. One may, of course, adopt the view of process theology which endeavors to provide for some change in God while it maintains his absolute transcendence. The fullness of the Holy Spirit celebrated in confirmation might refer to the change in God which process theology provides for. But if process theology allows for change in God, it does so to explain God's interaction with his creatures. So even process theology would very likely interpret the fullness of God's Spirit in terms of his fullness in us. This interpretation appears the most reasonable. "The fullness of God's Spirit" means the penetration of the Spirit and his influence further into our lives and through us into history and nature.

The Rite Itself

This understanding of the Holy Spirit's fullness emerges from the rite of confirmation. In the invitation to prayer before the imposition of hands, the bishop urges the congregation to ask God "to pour out the Holy Spirit upon them [the candidates]" (RC, n. 24). This request evokes the image of water poured out upon the ground and sinking down into it. The purpose of this outpouring of the Holy Spirit upon the confirmed is

> to strengthen them in their faith,
> and anoint them to be more like Christ the
> Son of God (RC, n. 24).

Like steel rods thrust into concrete, the Spirit is to penetrate into the faith of the confirmed to reinforce it. That
the confirmed may be more like Christ, the Spirit is to
penetrate their being, as ointment penetrates the flesh to
heal wounds or to make muscles supple, and as cold
cream penetrates the skin to beautify it.

As the bishop imposes hands on all the candidates, he
entreats God to send his Holy Spirit upon them "to be
their Helper and Guide" (RC, n. 25). The power and
the wisdom of the Holy Spirit are not to remain closed
up within the godhead but are to be extended into the
lives of the confirmed, enabling them for action and
directing their activity.

The bishop then begs God to give the candidates the
so-called seven gifts of the Holy Spirit:

> *Give them the spirit of wisdom and under-*
> *standing,*
> *the spirit of right judgment [counsel] and*
> *courage [fortitude],*
> *the spirit of knowledge and love [piety],*
> *the spirit of reverence in your service [fear*
> *of the Lord] (RC, n. 25).*

The seven gifts sought of God are qualities in man: the
spirit of wisdom and understanding, the spirit of right
judgment and courage, etc.

These seven gifts, moreover, are not an exhaustive
catalogue of what the Holy Spirit gives to those who are
open to him. Seven is traditionally a symbolic number; it
signifies perfection, completeness, fullness. Implied in
this prayer, then, is a request for all that the Holy Spirit
can bestow on men and women to enrich their lives as
human beings and as sons and daughters of God. The

prayer seeks the Holy Spirit's fullness in us so that our lives may be rich with the richness of the Spirit of Christ.

When the bishop makes the sign of the cross with chrism on the forehead of the candidate, he says: "Paul [or whatever the candidate's name], receive the seal of the Holy Spirit, the gift of the Father" (RC, n. 27). In these essential words of the sacrament of confirmation, "seal" alludes to Ephesians 1:13: "You too have been stamped with the seal of the Holy Spirit of the Promise, the pledge of our inheritance." "Gift" refers to Acts 2:38, where Peter tells the crowds at Pentecost that, upon being baptized, they will receive "the gift of the Holy Spirit." In Acts 10:45, the Jewish believers discern that the "gift of the Holy Spirit" has been given to Cornelius and his companions. A note in the foreword to the English text of the *Rite of Confirmation* states that "Gift" is capitalized in the formula of the sacrament to indicate that what is given is the Holy Spirit himself, the divine Person promised and sent by the Father through the risen Christ (Luke 24:49; John 14:26; 15:26; Acts 1:4-5; 2:33).

The use of chrism, of course, relates confirmation to Christ's "anointing" by the Holy Spirit, whereby he is God's beloved or only Son, as was manifested at his baptism in the Jordan. The Spirit of Christ is the source of our adoptive sonship in relation to the Father (Rom. 8:14-17; Gal. 4:6-7).

The sign of the cross made on the forehead of the candidate indicates that the Holy Spirit who is given is the Spirit of Christ, that he is given because of Christ's death and resurrection and that by his presence in us we are "marked" or "sealed" as belonging to Christ.

In the formula of anointing, the word "receive" is

the translation of *accipe,* a Latin imperative. The bishop, therefore, commands the candidate, or urges him paternally in the most earnest way possible, to "receive the seal of the Holy Spirit." Since the word seal is not capitalized, it refers to the anointing with chrism in the form of the cross. This bodily anointing is the outward symbol of the interior "anointing" with the Holy Spirit, that is, the Holy Spirit's entering more fully into the life of the candidate. The bishop appears to enjoin the candidate to receive the bodily anointing with chrism. But this can be only a superficial meaning of the words, for as the bishop says the words he is already anointing the candidate who has already come forward showing his openness to being anointed. There is no need to command him to be anointed bodily.

The meaning of the bishop's injunction, then, is that

the candidate should receive the Holy Spirit into his life. He should welcome into his life, as helper and guide (so described in the prayer at the imposition of hands), the Gift of the Father, namely, the divine person who is the Holy Spirit. He should let his life be influenced thoroughly (sevenfold gift) by the Holy Spirit in a person-to-person relationship. He should soak up the influence of the Holy Spirit as the earth soaks up water poured out upon it and as the flesh absorbs ointment (as implied in the invitation to prayer for the imposition of hands).

The bishop is saying to the candidate: "Receive the Holy Spirit's fullness in us; take advantage of the power and wisdom of the Holy Spirit whose help and guidance have been made available to you by his personal presence in you as a result of your baptism."

Thus confirmation does not celebrate a reality substantially different from that which baptism celebrates — the gift of life in the Holy Spirit. But confirmation perfects or completes baptism by celebrating more explicitly and emphatically the Spirit's role in that life and the consequent richness and possibilities of it.

But does not confirmation bestow the Holy Spirit for some specific purpose for which baptism does not equip us? Does confirmation not make us capable, as baptism does not, of participating in eucharistic worship, or of bearing witness to Christ, or of sharing in the Church's mission, or of partaking uniquely in Christ's priestly, prophetic, or kingly ministry?

The Christian community's liturgical rites express fundamentally for everyone the mysteries of Christian life which the community celebrates. The rites of confirmation and baptism do not indicate that confirmation is the celebration of the bestowal of the Holy Spirit for some specific purpose unprovided for in baptism.

In the prayers of the rite of confirmation, we can single out the following petitions as expressing what the sacrament is generally thought to celebrate most distinctively. The Christian community asks that the Holy Spirit may strengthen the candidates in their faith and make them more like Christ (RC, n. 24); that they may have the seven gifts of the Holy Spirit (RC, n. 25); that they may be witnesses to Christ (RC, n. 30); that they may have the courage to profess the true faith (RC, n. 33A) and may never be ashamed to proclaim Christ crucified (RC, n. 33B).

But in the rite of baptism we find equivalents for all

these petitions. The baptismal rite contains petitions that the baptized may be strengthened by Christ (RB, n. 50) and grow strong as living members of the Church (RB, n. 217); implied in these requests is strengthening in faith. The petition for the gifts of the Holy Spirit is implied in the prayer that the baptized may grow to be mature Christians in all the fullness of Jesus Christ (RB, n. 248). There are petitions that the baptized may become more perfectly like God's Son (RB, n. 223), more fully like Jesus Christ (RB, n. 247); and that they may be witnesses (RB, nn. 47, 217, 220) and proclaim the faith (RB, n. 65) and the Good News (RB, nn. 218, 224).

The other prayers contained in the rite of confirmation and in the Mass of confirmation could be offered with equal fittingness for the baptized, except for four clear but general references to the sacrament of confirmation.

In all the prayers of the rite of confirmation and the Mass for it, three themes stand out: greater likeness to Christ, witness and unity. As we have seen, the first two are found also in the baptismal rite. The theme of unity is also in the baptismal rite's references to the one people of God (RB, n. 224) and to life in the unity of faith and love (RB, nn. 217, 220).

But perhaps the time when confirmation is celebrated indicates that confirmation bestows the Holy Spirit for a specific purpose not provided for by baptism. In some places the ancient practice of conferring confirmation before the first reception of the eucharist is still in vogue. This practice may imply that confirmation celebrates a gift of the Spirit which is not given in baptism and without which a person is not capable of participating in the eucharist. This theory, however, like all the other theories which assign to confirmation some utterly unique gift of the Spirit, clashes with the facts of life. Baptized but unconfirmed Christians do participate in the eucharist just like confirmed Christians, as far as we can see. Unconfirmed Christians grow more like Christ, bear outstanding witness, live in the unity of faith and love and zealously participate in the life and mission of the Church. They often leave confirmed Christians far behind in the fullness of their personal and ecclesial Christian lives.

We may make all these activities the unique results of confirmation. We may assign them to confirmation as a bestowal of the Spirit for a purpose distinct from his bestowal at baptism. We may attribute them to spiritual powers given to the confirmed but not the baptized. We may declare their presence in the unconfirmed an exceptional gift of God. But these postulates belittle baptism, conflict with the facts of life, involve unnecessary and unverifiable hypotheses and reduce the credibility of the claims for confirmation.

The Church's official teaching about what it celebrates in confirmation and expects from it beyond baptism is very general. That teaching is summed up in Vatican II's statement that "by confirmation the faithful are endowed with special strength and are bound more intimately to the Church so that they are more strictly obliged to spread and defend the faith by word and deed as true witnesses of Christ" (*Constitution on the Church*, n. 11). This teaching affirms a qualitative difference between the baptized and the confirmed. This qualitative difference and all the Church's official teaching on confirmation can be preserved, as will become evi-

dent in subsequent chapters, by the view that confirmation celebrates the same mystery as baptism does, namely, life in the Spirit, but explicitly and emphatically celebrates a facet of that mystery which baptism leaves in the shadows, namely, the Holy Spirit's fullness in us.

This view makes sense in the light of the history of confirmation. In the process of developing the liturgy around baptism in water, the Christian community became conscious of confirmation as one of the important elements in the Church's sacramental nature, that is, its being the visible manifestation of God's invisible grace among men, the mystery of Christ in us. The community developed the baptismal liturgy in order to make its members more explicitly aware of the many facets of the mystery celebrated in the simple rite of washing a believer in water in the name of Jesus or the Trinity. So it is not surprising that confirmation celebrates basically the same reality as baptism does, but stresses an aspect of it which baptism does not.

Likewise it is not surprising that confirmation is conferred only once in a lifetime. The single conferral of baptism celebrates the irrevocableness of God's offer of life in the Spirit. It celebrates also complete union with Christ in his once-for-all death and resurrection which is the source of that offer and that life. So confirmation's once-for-all conferral celebrates God's unceasing offer of the Spirit's fullness in us. It also celebrates union with Christ in his single death and resurrection, which is the motive of God's offer and the origin of the Spirit's fullness in us.

The interpretation of confirmation which has been offered here may appear to reduce the difference between confirmation and baptism to a difference in symbolism.

Does confirmation not do something that baptism does not? Does confirmation not have its special effects or results? Yes, it does, and we shall be considering them in the next three chapters.

Chapter Four

Growth
in the Life
of the Spirit

Sandra doesn't know why she said it. She was playing bridge with her friends yesterday afternoon. The conversation turned to some nasty talk about the Jewish family who lives down the block. Sandra doesn't consider herself a model Christian. She goes to Mass on Sunday and does the standard things which Catholics do, but she is no Cursillista or charismatic enthusiast. She keeps her religion pretty much to herself. She does her share of gossiping, too. But she respects people and, in recent years, has become more aware of prejudice. So now she is often uncomfortable with the drift that gossip sometimes takes. Yesterday afternoon she grew very uneasy with the slurs being made on Jews. Suddenly she said, "I don't think Jesus Christ would talk like this." For 60 seconds the bridge game came to a halt. Even she didn't believe that she had said it.

Why did Sandra say it? The answer "because of her confirmation" will raise many skeptical eyebrows. Her confirmation occurred 15 years ago when she was a girl in seventh grade. Her life was not notably different after the event. She did not start calling her companions' attention to Christian values. To attribute yesterday afternoon's statement to her confirmation is absurd.

It is also unreasonable, however, to insist that Sandra should have begun to call people's attention to Christian values in the hour or the day after she was confirmed 15 years ago. Both opinions assume that the sacraments function in our lives mechanically or biologically rather than humanly.

How Confirmation Influences Life

The results of confirmation do not flow into our lives as electricity flows into the light bulb when we flick the switch on the lamp. Nor does confirmation affect our lives as quickly and surely as our glands' secretions influence our body's condition. Confirmation has its impact on our lives more in the manner of movies, TV programs and conversations with friends. The influence of these things on our views, values and choices is undeniable; but we feel and notice it only over the course of time, along with many other influences, and in some experience which brings it to the surface.

Our human life, as we know it from the inside, so to speak, is not the uniform running of a machine, the blind vital process of a plant or the instinctual reactions of an animal. It is a flowing, absorbing, whirling, flooding stream of sensations, feelings, images, emotions, questions, insights, ideas, searchings, reasonings, judgments, evaluations, decisions and actions. To some extent our "self" is carried along by this stream as a canoeist is almost helplessly carried down the rapids. To some extent we control the content of the stream. We limit the sensations we have, admit some images into consciousness and avoid others, surrender to feelings and emotions or temper them, pursue some questions and ignore others, attend to certain ideas and judgments and neglect certain ones, struggle with some decisions and never get around to others, engage in these activities rather than those. By controlling the content of the stream of our personal life, we control to some extent its direction.

Through his Word incarnate, Jesus Christ, God offers new content and direction for the stream of our life. This new content and direction are injected through preaching, the Scriptures, the sacraments, the teaching of the Church, catechesis, the witness of Christians in word and deed. Absorption of this content into our life stream gives life a Christian quality and direction; human life becomes also Christian life. Thus Christian life is a gift; it is grace, for its ultimate origin is not from within our individual selves, the community of man or nature, but the Word of God incarnate, Jesus Christ.

To live Christian life continually, we need to renew repeatedly the images and emotions, judgments and values, decisions and actions which make life Christian. For a more thorough and vigorous Christian life, we need to absorb that content more completely into the stream of our lives; and we need to add new content: more extensive familiarity with the biblical images by which God reveals his will; further discipline over more of our emotions; moral evaluations of our actions in additional spheres of our lives; new decisions about neglected aspects of our behavior.

The sacraments cause Christian life — or Christian life is an effect or result of the sacraments — insofar as the sacraments inject, renew and expand in the stream of life the contents which give life a Christian coloration and orientation. The sacraments perform this service by celebrating Christian life. By symbolic words, actions, things, images and personages, the sacraments heighten consciousness of the factors which make up life in the Spirit of Christ. More aware of these factors, we discern their values and are attracted to making them the values which guide our everyday lives. In this way the Spirit of God infuses Christian content and direction into the stream of our lives initially or more intensely or more extensively.

Thus Christian life depends upon the sacraments. Ultimately it depends on God's word in Jesus Christ. Jesus Christ is the source of the contents and direction of life in the Spirit. Jesus' presence is mediated to us by the sacraments. Hence, the sacraments are said to confer *ex opere operato* ("by their performance") the grace of Christian life. This expression means that the sacraments mediate to us the word of God in Christ which, when assimilated, makes life Christian. The sacraments' effectiveness is in their performance, not as human activities but precisely as conveyors of God's word in Jesus Christ.

The sacraments are not the only sources of Christian life. Christian content and direction in the stream of life result also from reading the bible, meditating on Jesus, praising and petitioning God in prayer alone or with others, hearing a sermon, studying theology, witnessing the Christian life of other people, reading certain poems, attending certain plays — any activity which somehow conveys to us the word of God. To the degree in which these activities bring the truth and beauty of the word of God into our awareness, they too may be said to foster Christian life *ex opere operato,* not because of what they are as human activities, but because they convey the word of God to us. The sacraments, however, along with Scripture, are paradigmatic conveyors of God's word and hence paradigmatic sources of Christian life. The other conveyors and sources find in the Scriptures and the sacraments their model and norm. These other carriers and sources cluster round the Scriptures and the sacraments to support, promote and diffuse their influence in our lives.

It is not so absurd, then, to attribute to her confirmation Sandra's speaking out yesterday afternoon. Her Christian witness derived from many sources. Among them were her natural respect for persons and her recently acquired sensitivity to prejudice. Other experiences, such as her regular participation in Sunday Mass and the "other things which Catholics do," sustained and carried into yesterday the values impressed upon her in her confirmation 15 years ago. She may have spoken out as she did even if she had never been confirmed. But as a matter of fact she was confirmed. That event was one of the many past experiences which fed Christian content and orientation into her life. All these experiences together made Sandra to be the unique person she was yesterday afternoon. Her confirmation was one of these experiences. Hence it was one of the reasons why she spoke out as she did.

Dispositions for Confirmation's Influence

As we noted, Christian content and orientation do not enter into the stream of life from the sacraments or Scripture as inevitably as electricity enters into a light bulb's filament or glandular secretions enter into the body. Our senses, imaginations, and minds must be open and attentive to receive them. Our emotional dispositions and above all our wills must be ready to accept them and act in accord with them. Hence the actual results of the sacraments are conditioned by the dispositions of those who participate in them. The content and orientation of life in the Spirit do come from the sacraments as bearers of God's word. But the degree of their absorption into the stream of life depends upon the recipients' alertness of faith and their readiness to love. The recipients' faith and love are conditioned, in turn, by the faith and love of the minister and the community, especially those close to the recipients, like their parents and teachers.

That Sandra's confirmation fifteen years ago made no noticeable difference in her life at that time is attributable quite possibly to the Christian community's lack of a vigorous life in the Spirit and its failure to provide her with an apprenticeship in Christian witness appropriate to confirmation.

Gradual Emergence of Effects

The full effects of the sacraments are not immediate. The intake or renewal of Christian content and direction may occur at a low degree of attention and readiness to act upon them. We may not be in the mood for a particular sacrament and may think that we are not deriving much benefit from it. But the content does enter into the stream of our lives. As symbolic activities, the sacraments affect us at deeper levels of consciousness than explicit awareness. Only afterwards, in appropriate circumstances, this subconsciously assimilated content comes to our attention and we act upon it. The sacraments influence us as does a conversation with a friend.

We do not immediately notice everything which a

friend tells us. Our attention is directed to one theme of the exchange so that we miss the significance of some of his statements. Nevertheless, we assimilate in memory very much of the conversation — the words spoken, various tones of voice, accompanying facial expressions. Afterwards, when we are reflecting on the meeting or when we are questioned by someone about the friend, we recall remarks which he made but which, at the time, we did not attend or react to.

On the other hand, from a sacrament we may attentively assimilate Christian content into the stream of our life and firmly resolve then and there to act in accord with that content, but the opportunity to act may not be at hand. When the opportunity comes, we may get "cold feet." Our conscience tells us what we should do because of our sacramentally derived awareness of the nature of Christian life and our resolve to act in accord with it; but we do not act. At some time or other, however, the opportunity to act comes; the force of our awareness and resolve, initially gained from the sacrament, overrides our fears, and we act in accord with the meaning of the sacrament for our Christian life.

Sandra did not begin to call people's attention to Christian values immediately after her confirmation or very often during the years that followed. But this failure to act is no reason to deny that her speaking out at the bridge game was due, in part, to her confirmation. A new opportunity to act in accord with her confirmation had arrived. The impact of her confirmation on her life had been sustained, at least minimally, over the years by her Sunday eucharists and other Christian activities. Now the circumstance of her disgust with nasty gossip triggered the release of her confirmation's influence and she spoke out. The fact that she was not explicitly aware of her confirmation's influence at the moment she spoke out does not negate the reality of that influence.

Hence, the effectiveness of the sacraments, including confirmation, cannot be judged on the basis of immediately noticeable changes in our lives. It can be judged only on the basis of their quality and direction over a long period of time. The ineffectiveness which we are prone to ascribe to the sacraments is not due to their lack of power to inject into the stream of life and to reinforce in it Christian content and orientation. Their apparent ineffectiveness is due to our lack of openness to God's word in Jesus Christ present to us through the sacraments; or it is due to our failure of nerve to act upon the content which we receive from them; or it is due to the absence of an opportunity to act.

We have been considering *how* the sacrament of confirmation and other sacraments cause life in the Spirit or how that life is an effect or result of confirmation and other sacraments. Now we turn to a consideration of *what* the effects or results of confirmation are. We begin with an effect of confirmation which it has in common with other sacraments when they are received by someone who is already living in the Spirit of Christ. This effect is an increase in that life.

Growing in the Spirit's Life

When new content of any kind enters into the stream of life, it causes an adjustment in the content already there and affects the direction of our lives. If we meet an attractive person and fall in love, for example, we give less thought to other old friends and spend less time with them.

Christian life, like life generally, is a dynamic whole consisting of many interrelated components, aspects and developments. An impact at any point on Christian life affects the whole of it. If one component, say faith, is strengthened, other components are strengthened: hope, love, humility, devotion. If one aspect is neglected, others will be also; failing to die to sin, we fail to live virtuously. If we develop responsibility as a baptized Christian, we will be able to develop responsibility as a married Christian or an ordained minister. If we neglect responsibility as a married or ordained Christian, we will neglect our responsibility as baptized Christians.

Confirmation celebrates the Holy Spirit's fullness in us which we received in baptism. Confirmation heightens consciousness of the Spirit's infinite wisdom and power at our disposal; it makes us more aware of the rich Christian life which can be ours because of our baptism. Aware of these resources and possibilities and drawn by the promise of the rich life which they hold out, we are moved to be more sensitive to the influence of the Holy Spirit and to develop the potentialities of our Christian life.

This more conscious recourse to the Holy Spirit and reaching out toward the fullness of life which he offers cannot help but develop other aspects of our life in the Spirit. We will intensify our repugnance toward sin and increase our efforts to live by God's commandments. We will become more concerned about and involved in the life and mission of the Christian community. In a word, the sacrament of confirmation will cause a general, over-all growth in the life of the Spirit.

This growth involves both an expansion and an intensification of life in the Spirit. It entails expansion in the sense that the influence of the Spirit begins to extend into areas of life which it did not previously touch. For example, we become as concerned about the morality of our business practices or our vote in political elections as we have been about the morality of our sexual behavior. Growth in the life of the Spirit includes intensification of that life in the sense that the influence of the Spirit becomes more forceful and consistent in whatever area of life it is operative; we evaluate, choose and act more firmly and steadily on the basis of the Gospel rather than on merely human and often sinful standards. Of course, this expansion and intensification of the Spirit's influence in our lives is conditioned by our attentiveness and readiness and by the community's encouragement, support and example.

When we speak of the sacraments' increasing, strengthening, perfecting, expanding, intensifying God's grace received in baptism, we understand these words as referring to a change in us, not a change in God's gracious attitude, in his giving or in what he gives. The sacrament of confirmation, or any other sacrament, does not celebrate a greater divine graciousness, giving or gift than the sacrament of baptism celebrates. But the sacraments subsequent to baptism celebrate that same graciousness, giving and gift as penetrating more deeply and vigorously into our lives and thereby changing them so that they become more Christlike. Thus the increase, strengthening and the like are not on God's side but on our side.

To speak of confirmation, therefore, or any sacrament, as increasing, strengthening, perfecting, expanding or intensifying life in the Spirit in no way belittles the fullness and perfection of God's blessings bestowed in baptism. On the contrary, to use these terms in the sense just explained emphasizes the dignity of baptism. The whole of Christian life consists in the assimilation of the gift of the Spirit of Christ which that sacrament celebrates. All the other sacraments serve that assimilation and, therefore, serve baptism.

Confirmation well received, then, results in over-all growth in the life of the Spirit. But confirmation does not exist precisely for the purpose of nourishing life in the Spirit. For that end we have the eucharist. Moreover, the effect of general growth in Christian life does not distinguish confirmation from the other sacraments. More important are its special effects. The first of these special effects is an abundance of life in the Spirit.

Full Life in the Spirit

In the sacrament of confirmation the Christian community intends to alert its baptized members to the infinitely powerful and wise Spirit of God dwelling and active within them as part of their baptismal heritage. It aims at stimulating them to welcome more wholeheartedly the Spirit's influence into their lives so that they live in all respects by the Spirit of Christ as true adopted sons and daughters of the Father. The prayers, anointing with chrism and essential words of the sacrament of confirmation concur to signify the Holy Spirit's fullness in us. This fullness, we saw in Chapter 3, means that the Holy Spirit's influence penetrates deeply into our lives. We become more Christlike. We live Christian life in all its richness. Therefore, "the fullness of Christian life" aptly designates the primary special effect of confirmation.

But do not the other sacraments cause the fullness of

Christian life? They do, but indirectly. Penance, anointing of the sick, holy orders and matrimony celebrate life in the Spirit in particular situations. Their special effects are contrition for sin, courage in suffering, dedication in service, fidelity in love. These special effects are factors in the life of the Spirit which are necessary for Christian life in particular situations. But through their special effects, and thus indirectly, these sacraments cause the fullness of Christian life because an impact at any point on Christian life affects the whole of it.

Baptism, confirmation and the eucharist celebrate elements of Christian life which are always present, at least implicitly and subconsciously, as long as one is living by the Spirit. The three sacraments differ from one another because each one, by its particular combination of prayers, actions, things, images, personages and frequency, expresses emphatically different factors always present in the life of the Spirit. Hence, each makes us attentive and responsible to different constituents of Christian life. The special effect of each of these three sacraments corresponds, then, to what each celebrates about life in the Spirit.

Stated very concisely, baptism celebrates life in the Spirit as living in Christ for the Father in opposition to sin and death. It celebrates incorporation into the Easter mystery of Christ's death and resurrection. Its special effect is aptly summarized as being "dead to sin but alive for God in Christ Jesus" (Rom. 6:11). Confirmation celebrates life in the Spirit as the fruit of the Holy Spirit's fullness in us. It celebrates incorporation into the Pentecost mystery of Christ's outpouring of his Spirit upon his disciples. Its special effect is, compactly put, the fullness of Christian life. The eucharist celebrates life in the Spirit as continuing personal communion with Christ in the mystery of his death and resurrection. Its special effect is summed up as loving union with Christ — the whole Christ, head and members. Let us consider further each of these special effects.

Baptism's special effect — life in the Spirit as dead to sin but alive for God in Christ Jesus — includes the fullness of Christian life. But the baptismal celebration does not emphasize the indwelling Holy Spirit's fullness in us to which the fullness of Christian life corresponds. The rite of baptism stresses, rather, life in the Spirit as incorporation by faith (RB, nn. 58, 59, 60) into Christ, especially into his death and resurrection (RB, nn. 47, 54, 217, 223, and 60, the baptism itself with all its symbolism). Hence it celebrates Christian life largely in terms of death to sin or Satan or evil (RB, nn. 49, 54, 57, 62, 219, 221) and in terms of new life (RB, nn. 47, 53, 54, 56, 62, 70, 217, 219, 220, 223, 224, 247) in Christ (RB, n. 62) as adopted sons and daughters of God (RB, nn. 68, 218, 319, 223, 224) among his people (RB, nn. 41, 47, 62, 70, 217, 220, 223). Hence, death to sin and life for God in Christ, not precisely the fullness of Christian life, is attributed to baptism as its special effect. Baptism causes the fullness of Christian life indirectly, by causing life for God away from sin, which ultimately implies the fullness of Christian life.

Interestingly, the rite of confirmation and the Mass for confirmation make scarcely any reference to sin, except in stating the results of baptism (RC, n. 25), in a petition that we may never be ashamed to proclaim Christ (RC, n. 33B), and perhaps in the request to be brought by the Lord through every trial (Mass for confirmation, Prayer after Communion, A). Taking this sparcity of reference to sin into consideration along with the significance of the rite of confirmation as analyzed in Chapter 3, we see that confirmation impressively celebrates life in the Spirit, not precisely in its movement away from sin toward the Father, but in its intrinsic richness and boundless potentialities for life in Christ because it is aided and guided by the infinite Spirit of God. Hence, the fullness of Christian life is fittingly ascribed to confirmation as its special effect.

The eucharist is the Christian community's frequently repeated *anamnesis* (memorial-making-present) of Christ's sacrificial death and resurrection. It is in the form of thanksgiving to God at a religious meal in which the risen Christ, through the consecrated bread and wine, offers himself to us in his sacrifice for personal communion with him. Thus, the eucharist celebrates life in the Spirit as continuing personal communion with Christ in the mystery of his death and resurrection. Its effect is loving union with Christ and his members, the building up of the body of Christ, the Church. This loving union obviously includes being dead to sin and alive for God; it also includes the fullness of Christian life. Indeed, the eucharist is meant to nourish, by intimate communion with Christ, the life of his Spirit promoted in baptism and confirmation. Moreover, close study of the eucharist and its liturgy uncovers themes echoing baptismal and even confirmational themes. But the dominant note of the eucharistic celebration is life in the Spirit as continuing personal communion with Christ. That celebration's proportionate effect is love of Christ and his members. The eucharist causes the fullness of Christian life indirectly by causing that loving union with Christ and his members which entails fullness.

A word of caution. We have used a number of catch phrases to designate what baptism, confirmation and the eucharist each celebrates distinctively about life in the Spirit. Catch phrases have also been used to identify the special effects of each of the three sacraments. The purpose of these phrases is to help us get some conceptual hold on very elusive reality. What each sacrament in fact celebrates about life in the Spirit is more extensive and nuanced than our catch phrases suggest.

The same observation holds for the special effects. The sacraments are symbols highly charged with meaning not only for the intellect but also for the imagination, the emotions and even the subconscious. They are events in that flowing, absorbing, whirling, flooding stream which is life where everything affects everything else and it is not easy to mark boundaries. Our tidy descriptions are no substitute for the experience of the sacraments' celebration and their influence on our lives, but only clues to help us profit more from the experience.

The phrase "the fullness of Christian life" has been used to designate the primary special effect of confirmation. Our next step is to unpack the meaning of that phrase and thus see in greater detail what the primary special effect of confirmation is.

Chapter Five

The Fullness of Christian Life

after Pope John XXIII had called for Vatican Council II, he was discussing with a Vatican official the necessary preparations. The official told Pope John that it would be impossible to begin the Council in 1963. "Then we'll begin in 1962!" Pope John replied.

Pope John's response, in its wit and its boldness, epitomizes his humanness and holiness. *The Journal of a Soul,* a collection of the pope's written reflections on his life, reveals a man close to God and led decisively by God's Spirit rather than by merely human motives. He lived a deep life of prayer. His love extended to men of every race, nationality, culture and ideology. It embodied St. Paul's description of Christian love: it was patient and kind, without jealousy; it never put on airs and was not snobbish, rude, self-seeking, prone to anger, or inclined to brood over injuries; it did not rejoice in what is wrong but rejoiced with the truth wherever it was found, even among atheists; there was no limit to its forbearance, its trust, hope and power to endure (cf. 1 Cor. 13:4-7).

Pope John's goodness, a Christian goodness, attracted all men: Protestants, Jews, Muslims, Hindus, Buddhists, humanists, atheists, Europeans, Africans, Asians, Americans. When he died, the whole world mourned his death. Pope John was a magnificent witness to the beauty and power of life rooted in faith in Jesus Christ.

Yet Pope John's holiness was not odd. It was very human. He was at home with a peasant as much as with a Vatican official. He visited sick friends. He did not like to eat alone. He enjoyed good food. He delighted in jokes and was ready with witty remarks. He was annoyed by pomp and protocol; he refused the first and broke the second. Pope John's holiness was the kind everybody was comfortable with.

"The fullness of Christian life" refers to holiness like Pope John's, to the deep prayer life and the generous love which are its principal elements, and to the moving Christian witness which flows from it. The task before us now is to see why and how this holiness, prayer, love and witness constitute the primary special effect of confirmation. At the same time, we will gain some understanding of these four constituents.

Holiness

The sacrament of confirmation celebrates the Holy Spirit's fullness in us, his influence in our lives. This influence grows, if we let it. A sign of the Spirit's influence in our lives is our attentiveness and responsiveness to the word of God, especially to the Word incarnate, Jesus Christ. The role of the Holy Spirit in the New Testament is to testify to Jesus (John 14:26; 15:25; 16:13-15; 1 John 5:6-7). The Spirit of truth (John 16:13) helps us to understand the mystery of Christ: Christ's fulfillment of the Scriptures (John 5:39), the meaning of his words (John 2:19), actions and the "signs" he performed (John 14:26; 16:13). The more we live by the word of God in Jesus rather than by the standards of mortal, fallen mankind, the more we are being led by the Spirit.

The influence of the Spirit can dominate all other forces in our lives: our instincts, temperament, character, education, intellectual ability, physical environment, social milieu, cultural heritage. The Spirit's impact will not do away with these other influences, but will dominate among them, control, modify and direct them. Our very human lives, each unique and shaped by a multitude of forces, will be shaped finally by the word of God. They will be molded into a following of Christ, whatever else they may be: the life of a factory worker or farmer, a secretary or business executive, a layman or a pope like John XXIII.

Theologians have a name for life dominated by the Holy Spirit. They call it mystical life. When we hear "mystical life" we tend to imagine some hooded monk or veiled nun staring blankly off into space, rapt in some interior vision. Or we imagine Bernini's statue of a swooning St. Teresa of Avila. St. Teresa, who was a no-nonsense, practical, busy woman, would have been embarrassed by Bernini's statue of her. The mystical life is simply life dominated by the influence of the Holy Spirit. Visions, voices, ecstasies and swoons that may occur can be explained in various ways, from the weakness of the psyche to gifts of God for edification. In any case, St. John of the Cross advises, they should be regarded with detachment. They are unessential to life in the Spirit and of secondary value at best. If they are from God, they will achieve their purpose without our bother. If they are from demonic forces, they will not harm us if we do not fix our hearts on them.

The mystical life is not to be confused with the contemplative life. The contemplative life is a style of living, like that of Carthusian monks, for example. It provides ample opportunity for silence, reflection and prayer. It aims at reaching contemplation, that is, deep prayer, which is an element in mystical life. But contemplation and the mystical life are not found only in the contemplative form of living. They are found also in the active style of life. St. Vincent de Paul was busy from dawn to nightfall caring for the needs of galley slaves, the poor and the religious organizations he founded. Yet he lived the mystical life as much as St. John of the Cross who was a Carmelite friar leading a contemplative form of life. What constitutes mystical life is the predominant influence of the Holy Spirit in one's life, be that life contemplative or active in style.

Theologians understand the mystical life to flow from the seven gifts of the Holy Spirit. They think of these gifts as oppenness to various influences of the Spirit. This openness is rooted in the love of God. We are easily influenced by those whom we love; and the more we love, the more readily we are moved. Because of our love for a friend, we are more apt to understand what he says than someone who merely knows him and has no particular affection and sympathy for him. We are also more inclined to follow the wishes of someone whom we love, rather than the wishes of someone whom we do not. To the degree that we love God, we are inclined to understand him and his ways and to do his will.

The gifts of the Holy Spirit, then, are love's openness

to God's influence. They are gifts *of the Holy Spirit* because God influences us through his Spirit within us. They are seven, a number symbolic of perfection, for love's docility to the influence of the Spirit is whole-hearted, reaches into every aspect of life and is limited only by the inspirations of the absolutely sovereign Spirit, who blows where he wills (cf. John 3:8). Mystical life is the activation of this openness to the influence of the Holy Spirit. It is beyond merely virtuous living, the so-called ascetical life, in which human reasoning, standards and efforts are still the predominant influences, even though guided by faith in the word of God.

In the rite of confirmation, immediately before the sacramental anointing, the bishop, on behalf of the Christian community, prays God to send the Holy Spirit upon the candidates as their helper and guide and to give them the seven gifts of the Holy Spirit. The subsequent anointing with chrism symbolizes the Holy Spirit's influence penetrating into the life of the one being confirmed, activating the gifts. The essential words accompanying the anointing command or urgently exhort the one being confirmed to receive the personal influence of the Spirit into his life. Thus in the sacrament of confirmation, the Christian community celebrates life in the Spirit as nothing less than mystical life and encourages its baptized members to live it.

To say that the primary special effect envisioned by the sacrament of confirmation is mystical life may "turn us off" because we have distorted popular ideas about mystical life, or because we think such life is utterly beyond any expectations which we may legitimately entertain for ourselves. But, as we have seen in the example of Pope John and in the theology of mystical life, that life is not so odd. It is simply the dominance of the Holy Spirit in our lives, our seriously living by the word of God, our wholeheartedly following Christ. To avoid the adverse reactions which "mystical life" evokes, we can use other terms which, though different in connotation, point to the same reality. Such other terms are "the fullness of Christian life" or "holiness."

The fullness of Christian life or holiness should not be beyond our expectations, for we are called to it by God's word. *The Constitution on the Church* of Vatican Council II reminds us that

The Lod Jesus, the divine teacher and model of all perfection, preached holiness *of life to each and every one of his disciples, regardless of their situation: "You therefore are to be perfect, even as your heavenly Father is perfect" (Matt. 5:48). . . . Thus it is evident to everyone that all the faithful of Christ of whatever rank or status are called to* the fullness of Christian life *and to the perfection of charity (n. 40, emphasis added).*

The Christian community celebrates the sacrament of confirmation for its baptized members precisely to make them aware that the Spirit's fullness is in them, so that the fullness of Christian life or holiness should not be beyond their expectations, but they should strive for it.

Deep Prayer Life

A prominent part of holiness is a life of prayer, like Pope John's. We say "life of prayer" and not simply "prayer." Holiness includes not only prayers at certain times but a persistent prayerful attitude, which inclines us to be at least subliminally conscious of God all our waking hours and which prompts us to occupy our thoughts with him frequently. "Prayer," moreover, means not only asking God for what we or others need and desire, though the value of petition should not be underestimated. Prayer is also praising and thanking God for his works and his gifts to us. The prayer life which is part of holiness is deep. It is deep objectively, for it is growing understanding of the mystery of Christ; it is grasping fully "the breadth and length and height and depth of Christ's love" and experiencing "this love which surpasses all knowledge so that you may attain to the fullness of God himself" (Eph. 3:18-19). It is deep subjectively, for it is the "full grasp" (cf. Eph. 3:18) of the plenitude of Christ's love.

A deep life of prayer is attributed to the Holy Spirit. "At every opportunity pray in the Spirit, using prayers and petitions of every sort" (Eph. 6:18). Through the Spirit of God's Son, Jesus Christ, we cry out "Abba!" ("Father!") (Rom. 8:15; Gal. 4:6). "The Spirit too helps us in our weakness, for we do not know how to pray as we ought; but the Spirit himself makes intercession for us with groaning that cannot be expressed in speech" (Rom. 8:26). Mystical theology attributes to the Holy Spirit, active particularly through the gifts of understanding, wisdom and knowledge, the insight into the mystery of Christ referred to in I Corinthians 2:6-16 and Ephesians 3:16-19.

In the rite of confirmation, the Christian community envisions a deep life of prayer for the baptized. The rite focuses on the Holy Spirit's fullness in us, the source of such prayer. The bishop invites the congregation to pray for the Spirit to strengthen the faith of the candidates. One way of strengthening faith is to clarify what is believed and what is not and to see its relevance. Thomas Aquinas (*Summa theologiae*, II-II, qq. 8-9) attributes such perfecting of faith to the gifts of understanding and knowledge. The bishop also invites the assembly to pray that the candidates may be anointed (with the Holy Spirit) to be more like Christ. Christ was continually in communion with his Father and often went apart from his disciples and the crowds to pray in solitude. Then, on behalf of the community, the bishop prays that the candidates may be given the gifts of love (piety) and reverence in God's service (fear of the Lord). With these two gifts mystical theology would associate living in awareness of God. The bishop prays also for the gifts of understanding, wisdom, and knowledge, to which mystical theology ascribes the most profound prayer. Finally, the bishop asks God to keep the gifts of his Spirit "alive" in our hearts, implying a deep life of prayer.

Such prayer expresses itself and is nourished in the liturgy, the common prayer of the Christian community. Confirmation intends, then, liturgical prayer as well as other forms. Moreover, historically confirmation entered the consciousness of the Christian community as part of the rite of initiation into the eucharistic liturgy.

Confirmation even foresees the possibility of unusual forms of prayer, such as "groanings that cannot be expressed in words" (Rom. 8:26), speaking in tongues, interpreting them, prophesying, having revelations (I Cor. 14:26-31). Insofar as it promotes a deep life of prayer inspired by the sovereign Spirit, confirmation cannot exclude the possibility of unusual kinds of prayer. More positively, the rite of confirmation admits their possibility. The sample homily for the rite of confirmation (RC, n. 22) mentions Paul's laying hands on the baptized, the

Holy Spirit's coming down on them and their speaking in tongues and prophesying (Acts 19:6). The sample homily (RC, n. 22) also says that the coming of the Holy Spirit in our day is "not usually" marked by the gift of tongues, implying that sometimes it might be.

Generous Love

A second major element of holiness is love of God and neighbor which goes beyond self-interest and duty. Vatican II's *Constitution on the Church,* in the passage cited above, speaks of all the faithful's call to "the perfection of charity." The two great commandments, said Jesus, are to "love the Lord your God with all your heart, with all your soul, with all your mind, and with all your strength," and to "love your neighbor as yourself" (Mark 12:30-31). The commandments, writes Paul, "are all summed up in this, 'You shall love your neighbor as yourself.' Love never wrongs the neighbor, hence love is the fulfillment of the law" (Rom. 13:9-10). Christian discipleship consists in mutual love: "This is how all men will know that you are my disciples: your love for one another" (John 13:35).

This love is not self-seeking (I Cor. 13:5) but, like Christ's, self-giving. It is self-giving toward God: "I [Paul] beg you through the mercy of God to offer your bodies as a living sacrifice holy and acceptable to God, your spiritual worship. Do not conform yourselves to this age but be transformed by the renewal of your mind" (Rom. 12:1-2). It is self-giving toward neighbor: "Love one another as I have loved you. There is no greater love than this: to lay down one's life for one's friends" (John 15:12-13). Self-giving love extends beyond friends: "You have heard the commandment,

'You shall love your countryman but hate your enemy.' My commandment to you is: love your enemies, pray for your persecutors" (Matt. 5:43-44). "Bless your persecutors; bless and do not curse them. . . . Never repay injury with injury" (Rom. 12:14-17).

Pope John embodied this outstanding love. He gave himself wholly to God and Christ in service to the Church and fellowmen, as his *Journal of a Soul* bears witness. He changed the wording of the prayer for the Jewish people in the General Intercessions of the Liturgy of Good Friday so that the prayer no longer stigmatized the Jewish people as faithless or perfidious. After four hundred years of estrangement between the Roman Church and the Church of England, he met with the Anglican Archbishop of Canterbury in Rome. Breaking with the custom of addressing papal encyclical letters only to the bishops, clergy and faithful of the Roman Catholic Church, he began with *Peace on Earth* to address them also to "all men of good will."

Confirmation envisions such Christlike love. The sacrament celebrates the Spirit's fullness in us. The first fruit of the Spirit in us is love, according to St. Paul (Gal. 5:22). The rite of confirmation prays for, symbolizes by anointing and urges in the accompanying words (RC, nn. 25, 27) the influence of the Holy Spirit in the candidates' lives through the seven gifts. This influence is radically through love for God, which includes love for neighbor (I John 4:21). In the General Intercessions of the rite, the deacon prays for the Christian people's growth in love and for the whole world's ability to see "beyond racial and national differences" (RC, n. 30). The bishop's final prayer over the people is that we may be ready to live Christ's gospel and be eager to do his will (RC, n. 33B); Christ's gospel and will are that we love God and neighbor. In the Mass for confirmation, a prayer over the gifts refers to the confirmed as offering themselves to the Father with Christ. Moreover, in the rite of Confirmation (RC, n. 25) the bishop prays for the gift of right judgment (counsel) and courage (fortitude). According to mystical theology, right judgment helps a person determine the loving action called for in a particular situation, and courage enables him to carry out the action despite any obstacles.

Moving Witness

Because confirmation promotes a deep life of prayer, its primary special effect includes witness. A deep life of prayer, expressing itself in a generally tranquil spirit, in private devotion, in communal liturgy and perhaps in unusual ways, like speaking in tongues, forcefully testifies to God's saving grace among men through faith in Jesus Christ. A second reason for confirmation's primary special effect including witness is the outstanding love which confirmation fosters. In the midst of widespread atheism, "what does the most to reveal God's presence . . . is the brotherly charity of the faithful . . ." (*Constitution on the Church in the Modern World,* n. 21). In the General Intercessions, the rite of confirmation refers to this witness through love; the deacon prays that the newly confirmed may be witnesses to Christ the Lord with faith and love as the foundation of their lives (RC, n. 20).

Love does not prefer one's own good but the welfare of the community. The love inspired by the sacrament of confirmation prompts the baptized members of the Church to work together unselfishly to build up the body of Christ. "Through him [Christ] the whole body grows, and with the proper functioning of the members joined firmly together by each supporting ligament, builds itself up in love" (Eph. 4:16). Thus confirmation, fostering the love which builds up the Church, promotes wholehearted participation in the Church's life, worship and mission by which witness is borne to Christ.

In the rite of confirmation, the bishop's final prayer over the people appropriately requests that we may never be ashamed to proclaim Christ crucified (RC, n. 33B); his final blessing prays for courage to profess the true faith (RC, n. 33A). A prayer after communion in the Mass for confirmation asks that those anointed with the Spirit and fed with the body and blood of Christ may build up the Church by their works of love. Another such prayer requests that those anointed with God's Spirit may live as prophets of his kingdom.

Complement to Baptism

The Holy Spirit's fullness exists in the baptized but unconfirmed person, of course, so that he or she can be holy, lead a deep prayer life, love unselfishly and witness forcefully to Christ in wholehearted participation in the life, liturgy, and apostolate of the Church. Some event or events other than confirmation can awaken a baptized person to the Spirit's presence and move him to avail himself of the Spirit's help and guidance for a full Christian life. Hence, we will not be surprised if we meet baptized but unconfirmed Christians who are profoundly good people, prayerful, generous in serving others and zealous in bringing the Good News to others by word and example. Baptism is sufficient for salvation, not simply in a minimal sense, but in a very full sense, for it entails the coming of the Spirit of God into our lives.

But the Christian community does not leave it to chance that its baptized members be alerted to the Spirit's fullness in them and to the fullness of Christian life which the Spirit's presence makes possible. The community has a public act in which it calls its baptized members' attention to the Spirit's fullness in them and to the holy, prayerful, loving and apostolic life which is theirs through his help and guidance. This public act is the sacrament of confirmation. By means of its regular performance, the Christian community ensures that those baptized in infancy and in adulthood are made conscious of the indwelling Spirit for intense Christian discipleship. Confirmation is celebrated even when a person is baptized as an adult, for confirmation complements baptism by calling attention to the indwelling Spirit's fullness with an explicitness and emphasis that are not present in baptism.

The Sacrament's Strength

As a result of the Christian community's public act of confirmation, the baptized, according to Vatican II, "are endowed by the Holy Spirit with special strength. Hence they are more strictly obliged to spread and defend the faith both by word and deed as true witnesses of Christ" (*Constitution on the Church*, n. 11).

The special strength referred to here consists, first, in the baptized person's being more highly conscious of the Spirit dwelling in him and of the fullness of Christian life to which he is called. Knowing better the help and guidance at his disposal, he can follow Christ with greater abandon and confidence. Seeing better the goal to which he is called, he can more certainly direct his actions toward it.

109

This strength consists, secondly, in a more vigorous inclination of the will toward the goal of Christian life and its chief means, namely, the power and wisdom of the indwelling Spirit. Confirmation not only heightens consciousness of what the goal and chief means of Christian life are, but also displays their beauty, value and desirability. Thus the goal and means are able to exercise more forcefully their power of attraction on the will.

This strength consists, thirdly, in the support which the Christian community gives to its baptized members in conferring the sacrament of confirmation on them. In preparation for confirmation and in following it up, the Christian community helps its members to understand more fully their baptismal heritage and vocation. It also shows them how they can live more intensely by this heritage and call. In the conferral of confirmation, the Christian community demonstrates to its baptized members its desire to have them live a full Christian life in its midst and to participate wholeheartedly in its life, worship and mission. The community's assistance and welcome strengthen a person in his following of Christ.

This special strength which confirmation confers constitutes another special effect of the sacrament. It pertains to the primary special effect of the sacrament. It is related to the fullness of Christian life as a beginning is related to the end. The special strength attributed to confirmation is the *proximate* primary special effect of the sacrament, for its emergence in one's life lies very close to the actual reception of the sacrament. The fullness of Christian life is the *ultimate* primary special effect of confirmation, for its emergence in one's life usually lies at some distance in time from the conferral of the sacrament. Insofar as the fullness of Christian life is definitively attained only in union with God beyond death, it may also be called the eschatological special effect of confirmation.

Because confirmed persons have greater awareness of what Christian discipleship entails, they are, in the words of Vatican II cited above, "more strictly obliged to spread and defend the faith both by word and deed as true witnesses of Christ." The baptized person is obliged to be a true witness of Christ, but the confirmed person is more strictly obliged because he knows more fully what the Christian vocation involves. This obligation, it is worth noting, is not externally imposed but arises from within. The confirmed person is more vividly conscious of the fullness of Christian life as an attainable goal through the influence of the Holy Spirit. He perceives more clearly the worth of that goal and its attainability. Thus he is more powerfully attracted to it. From within, then, he feels obliged, impelled, drawn to live as a true witness of Christ.

Other events in a person's life besides confirmation — such as a retreat, a scrape with death, association with an outstanding Christian — may also give special strength in following Christ and increase the obligation to Christian witness. The Holy Spirit is not limited to the sacraments in bestowing, sustaining or intensifying Christian life. But these facts do not invalidate Vatican II's assertion about confirmation's giving special strength and a more strict obligation.

Maturity

Confirmation has long been called the sacrament of matureness. The full development referred to is not physical, psychological or sociological; it is not a matter of bodily growth, of intellectual ability and emotional balance or of social awareness and responsibility. The maturity referred to concerns life in the Spirit. Confirmation celebrates the infinite power and wisdom of the sovereign Spirit within us as the source of Christian life. Such a source is certainly a perfection of power for Christian living. In celebrating the Spirit's fullness in us, confirmation makes us more explicitly conscious of the full or mature Christian life which he makes possible for us. As a result of confirmation, we are directed more explicitly and forcefully toward Christian maturity.

But celebration of the mature power for Christian life, greater awareness of that life's complete goal and orientation toward that goal do not mean necessarily that immediately after confirmation we begin to act as adult Christians. To put it in other words, the ultimate primary special effect of confirmation, namely, the fullness of Christian life, does not appear the hour or the day after conferral of the sacrament.

In view of what was said in Chapter 4 about the efficacy of the sacraments, we do not expect the ultimate primary special effect of confirmation to follow its celebration as a lighted lamp follows the flicking of a switch or a bodily change follows a glandular secretion. We expect that effect to follow confirmation as knowledge of a friend follows from a conversation recalled. Confirmation does inject into the stream of life new content: awareness of the Spirit's fullness in us and of the mature Christian life which he makes possible. Consequently, confirmation also influences the direction of life's flow. But this awareness and orientation issue in mature Christian acts of holiness, prayer, love and witness only as circumstances call them into full play. An attack on

Christian values calls forth our awareness, injected in us by confirmation, that the fullness of Christian life means unashamedly proclaiming Christ in such a situation. Our orientation toward Christian maturity, reinforced by confirmation, inclines us actually to bear witness to Christ. If we do not succumb to fear, we will speak out, and we will be doing so because of our confirmation, among other influences that may be at work.

As we go through life, we encounter numerous situations evoking the ideas and values which the Christian community, in its public act of confirmation, made us more aware of and inclined toward and which many other sources no doubt have nourished. We progressively acquire ease and satisfaction in acting on the basis of these ideas and values. We become increasingly mature Christians. The many-faceted effect of confirmation emerges in our lives. We approach the fullness of Christian life.

Development toward the realization of the ultimate primary special effect of confirmation is not likely to be uniform progress forward and upward, flowing solely from confirmation and personal effort. Development advances and then suffers setbacks, is sometime imperceptible, sometimes profound but slow, sometimes deep and rapid. We meet situations with mature Christian responses. In other circumstances we fail to act on the awareness and inclination which confirmation has implanted or reinforced in us. We do not make any genuine effort to pray; or, if we do, we find dryness and emptiness, become discouraged and give up the effort. We give in to selfishness. We do not stand up for Christian values. On the other hand, we have many aids: our fellow Christians' example and encouragement, the Christian community's eucharist and sacrament of penance, the word of God read, preached and pondered, retreats and days of prayer. Helps such as these coalesce with confirmation and personal striving. All together promote the eventual emergence of the fullness of Christian life, the fruit of the Spirit's fullness in us, which the sacrament of confirmation celebrates.

The rite of confirmation takes into account the gradual development, with help, of the sacrament's ultimate primary special effect. The bishop's prayer over the people asks the Father to "complete the work of love you have begun" (RC, n. 33B). The deacon prays in the General Intercessions for parents and godparents that they may encourage the newly confirmed to follow Christ (RC, n. 30). All the prayers for confirmation's effect, both in the rite and in the Mass of confirmation, presuppose the gradual emergence of the sacrament's special result. By its nature prayer looks to the future; and the realistic presupposition behind prayer is that the blessings asked of God will come about in accord with the nature of his creation, that is, in time.

Baptism of the Spirit

The development of the ultimate primary special effect of confirmation, we have noted, is sometimes very sudden and intense. Mystical theology speaks of "second conversion." The first conversion is a person's taking up Christian life. This first conversion may be a gradual process from infant baptism through basic catechesis to the kind of choice a child or youngster can make. The first conversion may also be a notable change in the life of an adult through faith sealed by baptism. On the basis of this first conversion, a person lives a generally virtuous life, striving to follow Christ according to the Gospel, but without particularly great enthusiasm. Then one day, for reasons as various as the individuals who have the experience, the person suddenly and profoundly becomes remarkably aware of what it means to be a disciple of Christ and begins to live a zealous Christian life. This change is the second conversion.

Theologians explain this second conversion as a breakthrough of the Holy Spirit's influence in the person's life. The Holy Spirit, through the seven gifts, becomes the predominant influence, more forceful than human reasoning, standards and inclinations, even those based on faith.

Comparable to this second conversion, and perhaps the same thing, is the "baptism of the Spirit" which is so important in the Neo-Pentecostal or charismatic movement. Those involved in this movement testify to a marked change in their lives resulting from a sudden and intense experience of the fullness of the Holy Spirit in them. This being suddenly gripped by the Holy Spirit is frequently accompanied by remarkable forms of prayer, such as speaking in tongues or interpreting them or prophesying or having a revelation. All of this is consistent with the theology of the Spirit's fullness in us which we have considered.

The first and fundamental baptism of the Spirit accompanies baptism with water. This baptism of the Spirit is the inner reality symbolized by baptism in water, imitative of Christ's baptism in the Jordan when the presence of the Spirit in him was manifested. The purpose of confirmation is to make the baptized members of the Christian community more fully aware of their baptism in the Spirit and its implications for their lives. This awareness and the direction it gives to life bear fruit in truly mature Christian holiness, prayer, love and witness only in the course of time, in response to appropriate situations and with various forms of help.

On some occasion, perhaps at a charismatic prayer meeting, this awareness and orientation may be provoked to action notably superior in maturity to previous activity. It may issue in profound prayer, "the Spirit himself [making] intercession for us with groanings that cannot be expressed in speech" (Rom. 8:26). The influence of the Holy Spirit begins to dominate in a person's life, manifesting itself in more generous love of neighbor, more bold witness to Christ and generally greater holiness, like Pope John's.

This change in Christian life is the result of the Holy Spirit's fullness in us. This fullness is celebrated explicitly and emphatically by the Christian community in confirmation. Hence, the change is fittingly regarded as part of the ultimate primary special effect of confirmation. However, the fullness of the Spirit is, as a matter of fact, the inner mystery of baptism; therefore, the emergence of the Spirit's influence as dominant in life is appropriately called baptism of the Spirit. It is, nevertheless, the second baptism of the Spirit, the flowering of the first. It can occur, of course, without the intervention of confirmation. Some other event may be the occasion for being seized more fully by the Holy Spirit's fullness in us.

The sacrament of confirmation envisions this second baptism of the Spirit whether it is accompanied by charismatic gifts or not. Confirmation seeks to promote the fullness of the Spirit in our lives. That intention includes the Holy Spirit's influence some day taking over our lives. This breakthrough of the Spirit as dominant will always be a profound personal experience. It may be associated with remarkable forms of prayer or wonderful gifts, like healing. The Neo-Pentecostal baptism of the Spirit, then, has roots in both the sacraments of baptism and confirmation. It is less dependent on the latter than on the former, however, for baptism is the primary and essential ecclesial celebration of the gift of the Spirit.

Commitment

Finally, confirmation is often called the sacrament of commitment. It is not the sacrament of commitment as penance is the sacrament of repentance or matrimony the sacrament of marriage. In penance and matrimony our graced activity — contrition in penance, the mutual promises of marriage in matrimony — enter into the very essence of the sacrament; they are the so-called matter of the sacrament. These activities of ours are "elevated" into the principal, public, paradigmatic grace-giving activities of the Christian community.

Our Christian commitment, however, is not the matter of the sacrament of confirmation. Confirmation does not elevate our commitment to the status of a sacrament. It does not celebrate life in the Spirit as committing self, but as issuing from the fullness of the Holy Spirit within. Confirmation celebrates directly and primarily the Spirit's activity in us and, as a consequence, our action as coming from his influence. This fact is revealed by the analysis which we have made of the rite of confirmation.

Commitment is a slippery word. What do we mean by it? We may mean by it a resolve to live earnestly the vocation of following Christ to which God, through the Christian community, calls us in baptism. The making of this commitment is envisioned by the rite of confirma-

118

tion as a predisposition for the sacrament. The rite provides for a renewal of baptismal promises before the conferral of confirmation (RC, n. 23). Confirmation is thus an *occasion* for commitment according to one's baptismal vocation, an occasion for personal ratification of one's baptism. But confirmation is not precisely the sacrament of commitment or ratification.

By *commitment* we may mean a wholehearted dedication to the fullness of Christian life which is not so much our resolve as the breakthrough of the dominant influence of the Holy Spirit in our lives. Commitment, in this sense, is a component of second conversion or baptism of the Spirit. This commitment is a result of confirmation, an element of the fullness of Christian life. In line with what we have said several times about the effect of confirmation, we do not necessarily expect to see this commitment occur the instant confirmation is conferred or even in the hours and weeks following it. This commitment may happen when the sacrament is received, but it more likely will occur at some unpredictable future moment: during a retreat, at a prayer meeting, in an encounter with a truly Christian person, in the face of death, or wherever the free Spirit of God chooses. Moreover, it will most likely occur only with the encouragement of the Christian community and with the help of all the means of grace at a person's disposal.

The Mystery of Pentecost

Christian theology has associated baptism with Easter and confirmation with Pentecost. Baptism celebrates life in the Spirit precisely as death to sin and life for God, as participation in the mystery of Christ's sacrificial death and resurrection by the power of the Spirit to

119

new life in the presence of the Father.

But Jesus not only rose by the power of the Spirit to new life in the presence of the Father. He also became, with the Father, the bestower of the Holy Spirit upon all mankind. This phase of the mystery of Christ was manifested on Pentecost, when the Spirit's influence began to dominate the lives of Jesus' disciples. When that happened, the disciples too became bestowers of the Spirit in the likeness of Jesus but as his ministers or servants. They began to preach the Good News (e.g., Acts 2:14-37; 3:12-26; 4:8-12). They began an intense life of prayer (Acts 2:42, 46-47), notable care for one another (Acts 2:44-45; 4:32, 34-35), and moving witness (Acts 2:47; 4:33; 5:13). In other words, they began to live the fullness of Christian life as a result of the Spirit's fullness within them, so that in the likeness of Jesus and as his ministers they conveyed the Spirit of the Father to men and women.

Confirmation, in celebrating the Spirit's fullness in us and in moving us toward the fullness of Christian life, celebrates the effects of our participation in the mystery of Pentecost, our serving Christ in communicating the Spirit of the Father to mankind. Other events in our lives may introduce us into the mystery of Pentecost, but confirmation is the Christian community's public, paradigmatic celebration of our participation in that mystery.

In summary of this chapter, the fullness of Christian life, the ultimate primary special effect of confirmation, consists of holiness with its two principal components of a deep life of prayer and generous love, and with its consequence of moving Christian witness, which entails wholehearted participation in the life, worship and mission of the Church. The proximate primary special effect of confirmation, which begins the development of the ultimate primary special effect, is a special strength which the sacrament confers. This special strength consists in heightened consciousness of the Spirit's fullness in us for a full Christian life, increased attraction to a full Christian life through the power and wisdom of the Spirit, and the Christian community's support in pursuit of the fullness of Christian life in the Spirit. These primary special effects of confirmation profoundly transform our personal lives in relation to God and our fellow human beings on this side of death and for eternity beyond. Confirmation also has a secondary special effect which pertains to us as members of the pilgrim Church. This ecclesial effect of confirmation will be the subject of the next chapter.

Chapter Six

Full Ecclesial Recognition of Adulthood in the Spirit

In the fall of 1971, I taught an adult education course on the sacraments. The class consisted mainly of people involved in CCD (the Confraternity of Christian Doctrine) for the religious education of the young. All participants were interested enough in a better understanding and appreciation of their faith to give their Monday evenings to the course and, occasionally, to brave cold fall rains to be there.

After a lecture on confirmation a woman raised her hand. "I don't see the necessity of confirmation," she said. "I'm a convert and have never been confirmed. Yet I don't see that my life is any less Christian. I don't feel that I'm missing anything."

Listening to her, I thought of the vast number of confirmed Catholics comfortably at home watching TV that Monday evening. Relatively few of them were interested in learning more about their faith and its significance for life in today's world. Even fewer of them were involved in any apostolate of the Church. This unconfirmed woman, on the other hand, was giving her time and

energy to these Monday evening lectures and was participating in the Church's teaching mission. Not only was
she not less Christian than so many of the confirmed; she
was more Christian. Was she, then, really missing anything? What would confirmation add to the life of this
woman?

Obviously confirmation would not add anything that
is absolutely necessary for vigorous life in the Spirit. The
Spirit is leading her to follow Christ in his death and resurrection. Evidence of the Spirit's influence is her everyday Christian conduct and her desire to know more fully
and to communicate to others the Good News. Perhaps
the Spirit's influence is not completely dominant in her
life; perhaps she has not experienced a second conversion
or the baptism of the Spirit; perhaps she has. In any
case, as far as we can judge, she has mature power for
the fullness of Christian life, namely, the Holy Spirit
dwelling within her; and she is well on the way toward
the fullness of Christian life. Moreover, the Father's gift
of the fullness of Christ's Spirit in her has been celebrated in her baptism so that she is clearly a member of the
Church in its visible manifestation. She also participates
regularly in the sacramental liturgy of the Church, especially the eucharist and penance, and in the mission of
the Church. So her Christian life in the Spirit has an appropriate ecclesial dimension. What could confirmation
add to all this?

To answer this question, we will consider this woman's Christian life in relation to the Christian community. Life in the Spirit is life in Christ. Life in Christ
means life as a member of Christ's body, the Church.
The answer to the question will be in terms of the woman's relation to the Church and its relation to her.

124

The Church: Community and Institution

When we look at the Church, we can perceive in it two aspects which are distinguishable even though they exist together and interpenetrate and overlap one another. We can see the Church as community and as institution.

The Church is community insofar.as it is persons interacting and cooperating with one another on the basis of commonly held beliefs and values. The purpose of their working together is to satisfy principally religious needs, but also other related human needs. Particularly noteworthy here is that the Church as community is people talking to one another, exchanging views, making decisions together, helping one another, worshiping jointly, working side by side, arguing with one another and often finally agreeing, hurting one another and being reconciled. The Church as community, *koinonia,* fellowship, is not an abstraction or merely an ideal. It is people getting their hands dirty together in the hard work of realizing God's reign in the world and, in the process, learning to respect, trust and love one another.

When people sharing common beliefs and values live and work together, they inevitably institutionalize their shared activities. They interact with one another in certain patterns. For example, there is an expected way for greeting a close friend and one for meeting a stranger. There is a pattern for producing useful goods, distributing them and selling them. In these patterns of interaction, people play different roles. In secular society there are public officials and plain citizens, merchants and customers, businessmen and farmers. In religious communities there are priests, laymen, catechists and catechumens.

People living and working together frequently draw

up statements of their common beliefs and values, of their expectations of one another, of the procedures they will follow in their joint life and work. Thus the beliefs and values uniting people in civil societies are expressed in constitutions of government, their mutual expectations in contracts, their procedures in laws. The unifying beliefs and values of people in Churches are expressed in creeds, their expectations in promises and their procedures in codes of canon law or Church order.

People seek to keep alive and foster the spirit which animates and unites them in their common life and work. They achieve this goal by regular celebrations of that animating and unifying spirit, for example, by parades and speeches on the Fourth of July or, in the case of the Christian community, by the Sunday liturgy of the Word and the eucharist.

Without institutions people would experience chaos rather than harmony in their life together. They would be as ineffective as a football team without any plays. They would be confused about who is and who is not a member of the community, about what is expected of each one, about the goals being pursued and the means to reach them. The set of beliefs and values which vivifies their life and work would eventually evaporate. So institutions are not bad. On the contrary, they are inevitable for people frequently interacting, necessary for easy and efficient cooperation and good for sustaining the life of the community.

The Church is institution, then, insofar as it is the Christian community organized for life and work together. The Church as institution does not exist apart from the Church as community or vice versa. The Church as institution is simply the organization in the

Church as community. Yet the Church as institution and the Church as community are not identical.

A sign of their nonidentity is the fact that the Church's institutions, as any community's, never cover the whole of the Christian community's shared life and work. People are constantly meeting one another in situations for which there is no accepted pattern of interaction. Creeds, like state constitutions, enunciate only the more prominent beliefs and values by which the community lives from day to day. Promises, like contracts, cannot foresee all the future circumstances which will affect the ability to carry them out. Codes of Church discipline, like civil laws, provide for normal life; they cannot envision all the oddities which life casts up. Institutionalized celebrations do not exhaust people's need to reflect on who they are, whence they have come and whither they are going; nor do they satisfy people's desire to experience one another's support.

Correlatively, the Christian community's life and apostolic efforts overflow its institutions. In living and working together, the Christian people are forever responding to new, unforeseen situations for which they have no agreed-upon patterns of behavior. They must act beyond their institutions according to the spirit which unites and inspires them until they manage to up-date old institutions or establish new ones. Thus the Church as community animates the Church as institution and develops it.

Another sign of the distinction between the Church as fellowship and the Church as institution is the fact that the former may languish while the latter goes on. Selfish, unloving Christians may constitute the majority of the Church's members. But babies will be baptized, children catechized, priests ordained, Sunday Masses attended, holy days observed. The reason for these activities will not be so much mutual love and the desire to build up the Body of Christ, but mainly the simple fact that they are the things to be done by members of the Church; they constitute the accepted pattern of life. Eventually, of course, these institutions will collapse and vanish if they are not supported by a renewed fellowship giving them genuine meaning and value. On the other hand, people may live and work together with profound Christian faith, hope, love and zeal, even though their institutions are inadequate or in some disarray because they are in the process of being reformed.

The distinction between the Church as community and as institution is not a distinction between invisible and visible aspects of the Church. The Church as community is visible, for it consists of human beings whose presence can be perceived, whose words can be heard, whose actions can be seen. The institutional Church, moreover, is not identical with the juridical Church, that is, the Church as ordered by law and legally recognized customs. The juridical Church is part of the institutional Church, but the latter is broader. Not all the institutions of the visible community's life have their origin from law or are sanctioned by law.

Hence, when we speak of the Church as institution, we do not intend to emphasize its visibility. That visibility is presupposed. We intend, rather, to stress the Church's organization. Further, we do not refer only or primarily to its fixed, legal organization, though that organization is not excluded. We refer to something broader, namely, the partially stable, partially developing complex of structures, roles and patterns of action and interaction which organizes the Christian fellowship in its life and work.

The sacraments belong to the Church as community. They are part of the Christian people's ongoing interaction and cooperation for the fulfillment of religious needs. The sacraments also belong to the Church as institution, for they are obviously organized interaction and cooperation. They are among the most important institutions of the Christian community. Along with the proclamation of the Word, they are regarded as paradigms of the community's activities, both organized and informal, emerging from, embodying and bearing witness to the grace of God among men.

Confirmation and the Church as Community

By the sacrament of confirmation, Christian people in community heighten baptized members' awareness of the Spirit's fullness in them and the fullness of Christian life which he makes possible; they also intensify the baptized persons' desire for Christian maturity. As a result, the baptized receive special strength consisting of that heightened awareness and intensified desire plus a sense of the community's support. Thus, they are helped to live by the Spirit in a way approaching ever closer to Christian maturity.

But a more mature life in the Spirit is lived within the Christian community. It involves greater interaction and cooperation with other people in Christian life and apostolate. Thus, confirmation's primary special effect entails a baptized person's deeper relation to the Church as community. This more profound incorporation into the Church as community consists primarily in greater love for, allegiance to and readiness to cooperate with the persons who make up the Christian community. Secondarily, it consists in engaging in more or different activities than before insofar as this is possible.

Correlatively, in conferring confirmation the Christian community expresses a new attitude toward the baptized person and so deepens its relation to him or her. The community says to the baptized: "Henceforth we will regard you as having the mature power of the Spirit within you for full Christian life; we will expect of you increasingly mature Christian conduct, and we will count on your exercising responsibility for our life and mission."

Even though the newly confirmed are physically, psychologically or sociologically still children or minors, the community acknowledges that they, by baptism, have the very power and wisdom of the Holy Spirit within them for mature Christian life and apostolate. The community also acknowledges its duty to help them actualize their potentiality as they enter into physical, psychological and sociological maturity. Thus the community deepens its relation to even the very young who are confirmed. It begins its deeper relation by acknowledging their possession of the mature power of the Spirit. It consummates that deeper relation over the years by involving them increasingly in the full life and mission of the Church as they attain physical, psychological and sociological maturity.

Returning now to the baptized but unconfirmed woman, we can say that she is already deeply related to the Church as community and vice versa. She is living an intense Christian life in her pursuit of personal holiness and in her considerable involvement with other people in Christian worship and apostolate. On the side of the community, people have recognized her Christian maturity in giving her responsibility in the community's teaching apostolate. Would confirmation deepen these relations existing between the woman and the Church as community?

Confirmation's general effect of over-all growth in the life of the Spirit (see page 88) would deepen her relation to the Church by intensifying her love for her fellow Christians with whom she interacts and cooperates. But the eucharist would have the same effect and exists precisely for the purpose of nourishing an ever deeper relation to the Church as community. Confirmation from the point of view of over-all growth in Christian life would contribute nothing special to her relation to the Church as community.

If we consider confirmation's proximate primary special effect of special strength (see page 109), we could argue that confirmation would deepen her relation to the Church as community, or at least modify her already deep relation. Obviously she already has special strength for Christian life and for community involvement derived from some one or several sources. But the sacrament of confirmation would give her an at least slightly different special strength. This special strength would not be due to some indescribable, mysterious power resident in the sacrament. It would come from the sacrament's symbolism which would make an impact on her consciousness, attract her desire and impress on her a sense of community support such as no other symbolic activity would. Thus she would be related to the Church as community in a way distinctive of confirmation.

Admittedly, it would be extremely difficult to put into words the precise difference between confirmation's special strength and consequent special relation to the Church on the one hand and, on the other, the special strength and relation derived from, let us say, a Bible service or a Mass liturgy celebrating the Spirit's fullness in us for full Christian life. Nevertheless, there would be a difference. Two novels having basically the same plot influence our awareness and desires differently and make different impressions upon us. Similarly, confirmation's celebration of Christian life as the fruit of Spirit's fullness in us will affect us and relate us to the Church as community in a slightly different manner than any other celebration of the same theme.

In regard to the relation of the Church as community to the woman, confirmation would deepen that relation in proportion to the people's attitude. If the people of the community confer confirmation on her simply because they feel that, for some unknown reason, they should, they are not going to deepen their recognition of her Christian maturity and their sense of obligation to her. They are not going to intensify their welcome of her as a mature Christian into their life and work. If, on the other hand, they understandingly, enthusiastically and lovingly celebrate for and with her the Spirit's fullness in her and the potentialities for the fullness of Christian life which he makes possible, then the Church as community will deepen its relation to her.

Confirmation and the Church as Institution

We have been considering confirmation as an activity of persons interacting and cooperating with one another because they share the same Christian spirit. Now we turn to confirmation as one of the institutions in their life and work as organized. What role does confirmation

play in the Church's organization, in the Church as institution?

Confirmation is one of the institutional Church's paradigmatic celebrations of life in the Spirit. It has its place with the proclamation of the Word and the sacraments. These celebrations are organized so that they occur at important moments in the life of the Christian community and throughout the life span of each member of the community. This set of celebrations serves to bring out fully to the consciousness of believers the various aspects of life in the Spirit which are necessary at all times and in certain situations. Thus these paradigmatic celebrations help believers to live always by the Spirit.

In this system of institutional celebrations, confirmation's distinctive role is to celebrate emphatically Christian life in all situations as the fruit of the Spirit's fullness in us through baptism. Confirmation complements baptism in the system. Confirmation, then, is institutional and, more particularly, official public recognition that a baptized person has the mature power of the Spirit in him or her through baptism and is called to the fullness of Christian life. It is institutional acknowledgment of the rights and duties which the baptized person has, as an adult in the life of the Spirit, to participate fully in the life and mission of the Church (whether this participation will occur immediately after confirmation or in the future in the case of a recipient who is still physically, psychologically or sociologically a child or minor). It is also official public recognition of the community's obligation to treat a baptized person as having maturity in the Spirit and, consequently, to help him or her live accordingly as he or she progresses through life.

Thus confirmation establishes a new relation of the

Church as institution to the baptized. By confirmation the organized Christian community stands as having recognized in an institutional way the baptized person as an adult in the Spirit (whatever his status may be in terms of physical, psychological or sociological adulthood). The community also stands as having acknowledged publicly its obligations toward him as mature in the Spirit. But the baptized person has a further relation to the Church as institution: he is now an institutionally recognized adult in the Spirit with the rights and obligations which that status entails in the institutional Church.

In regard to the unconfirmed woman, it may be difficult to say what confirmation would add to her life in relation to the Church as community. But it is not difficult to say what confirmation would add to her life in relation to the Church as institution. She has, indeed, the maturity of the Spirit in her and, being docile to his inspirations, is doing a respectable job of living an adult Christian life personally and communally. But as long as she remains unconfirmed, she lacks that official public recognition of her adulthood in the Spirit which the Christian community in its organized flow of life normally gives its members.

Practically speaking, this institutional recognition does not appear to be very important and is certainly not necessary, either for the individual or for the Christian community. For the individual, far more important and indeed necessary for Christian life is actually tending to the fullness of that life under the influence of the indwelling Spirit. Whether or not this status is publicly acknowledged is relatively immaterial. On the other hand, to be confirmed, to be institutionally recognized as having the mature power and wisdom of the Spirit at one's disposal, is of little significance if one is not living by that power and wisdom.

For the Christian community, important and necessary for its life and mission is that it have members truly living by the Spirit's fullness whether or not these members have been institutionally recognized as having the Spirit's fullness within them. Yet the Christian community benefits little by officially acknowledging that certain members have the maturity of the Spirit within them if the members do not follow the Spirit's inspiration and guidance or if the community does not help them to live by the Spirit.

Full Church Recognition of Adulthood

Nevertheless, the institutional recognition of one's possession of the Spirit's fullness and one's vocation to the fullness of Christian life does round out or complete one's membership in the Church. For the Church as the body of Christ is not only a fellowship of believers but also an organized community. One should have a place as mature in the Spirit, not only in the Church as community, but also in the Church as institution. In the Church as community, one has a place as an adult in the Spirit by living a maturing Christian life and by full involvement in the community's life and mission. But in the Church as institution, one can have a place as an adult in the Spirit only by confirmation because confirmation is the organized community's official public acknowledgment of maturity in the Spirit through baptism. Thus confirmation confers *full* ecclesial recognition of adulthood in the Spirit in the sense of rounding out or completing by an institutional act the recognition which the Christian people as community manifest in their daily welcome of the baptized person into their life and work together.

Full ecclesial recognition of adulthood in the Spirit is the secondary special effect of confirmation. It is a special effect of confirmation because confirmation alone confers it. It is secondary because it is less important than the ultimate and proximate primary special effects, namely, the fullness of Christian life and special strength for that life. These latter effects pertain to life in the Spirit insofar as it involves intimate union with the Father, Son and Holy Spirit in this life and in life beyond death; full ecclesial recognition of adulthood in the Spirit pertains to the position which one has in the institutional pilgrim Church.

Position in the Church

Full ecclesial recognition of adulthood in the Spirit gives the baptized person a place in the Church as institution. This place is distinct from that of the merely baptized person. The latter has the position of publicly and officially acknowledged membership in the organized Christian community. He is publicly and officially accepted and known as a member of the team. The ball can be thrown to him. He can receive all the sacraments and participate in the community's worship, parish councils and apostolic projects. He can be expected to carry the ball toward the goal of the community.

The confirmed person, in addition, is publicly and officially recognized as a member who is adult in the Spirit. He is accepted and known as belonging, not only to the team, but to the first string of players. The community expects him to be on the field for the game, not

137

sitting on the bench waiting to be called upon. He does not have the place of the coach, however; he is not an ordained bishop, priest or deacon.

The positions of the ordained bishop, priest and deacon are shares in the apostolic office, that is, the place of primary public responsibility in the Church for the welfare of the whole Christian community in its life and mission. This is a place of *responsibility,* of a call to serve Christ, the head, and his body, the Christian people, collectively and individually, as community and as institution. It is a place of *public* responsibility in two senses: (1) it is concern for the public welfare, for the over-all good of the whole people of God in all of its aspects, for the building up of the body of Christ in truth and love to "form that perfect man who is Christ come to full stature" (Eph. 4:13); and (2) it is responsibility publicly acknowledged by ordination, an act of the institutional Church. By ordination the whole community — bishops, priests, deacons, confirmed, and baptized — say to the candidate for holy orders that they acknowledge him as assuming, in answer to his personal vocation from God, responsibility for their over-all welfare. The apostolic office is a place of *primary* public responsibility, for although all members of the Church are responsible for its prosperity, lay persons fulfill that responsibility by attending to their particular tasks with the good of the whole kept in mind; and they are not the first ones held accountable for the general good by God and the people. But the ordained ministers' business is precisely concern for the over-all prosperity of the community and, because of that, also concern for the development of individuals. Moreover, the ordained ministers are the first ones responsible before God and the people for the vigorous life

and mission of the community.

The Sacrament's Character

Full ecclesial recognition of adulthood in the Spirit, giving a place in the Church as institution, also explains the so-called sacramental character of confirmation. Traditionally the sacraments of baptism, confirmation and holy orders have been understood to confer a character or mark or sign of some sort. The Council of Trent was reaffirming this tradition when it repudiated those who say that "in three sacraments, namely, baptism, confirmation and holy orders, a character is not imprinted on the soul, that is, a certain spiritual and indelible sign, so that they cannot be repeated" (Session VII, 3 March 1547, canon 9).

Theologians generally agree that the Council of Trent, in making this declaration, intended principally to affirm the fact that these three sacraments bring about some permanent effect, traditionally called a character; and because of that effect, these three sacraments are not repeated if they have once been validly received. The Council did not intend to define the precise nature of a character which was interpreted differently by various Fathers of the Church and theologians.

Both the Fathers of the Church and the theologians regarded the characters as results of baptism, confirmation and holy orders — results which endured even if one sinned and thereby ceased to live in the grace of God as called for by the sacraments. Because this result endured, it was like a stamp, a seal, a mark, a brand, a tattoo or, in the Greek language, a *character,* made upon some thing or some person. The Church, as a matter of fact, did not repeat these sacraments once they were validly received; a sinner was accepted back into the community through penance, but he was not baptized or confirmed or ordained again. St. Augustine pointed to the enduring character as the reason for not repeating these sacraments.

Among the Fathers of the Church, the idea that these three sacraments imprinted a character on the soul was a way of expressing the irrevocableness of God's love bestowed on a person through these sacraments. The recipient might reject God's love by sinning and thus cease to live in God's grace, but God's graciousness toward him did not cease. God is faithful to his covenant with a man. Having once given him his divine love, he continues always to watch over him, protect him from evil forces and assist him, if need be, to repent and return to life in the Spirit.

St. Augustine was the first to clarify the distinction between the character and life in the grace of God. For him the character was intimately related to, a kind of extension of, the external sacramental rite. Medieval theologians, however, transferred the character to an interior effect within a person and offered various understandings of this interior effect. The Council of Trent used the language of the medieval theologians to affirm the fact of the sacramental characters and their general qualities; but the council did not sanction the details of the medieval theologians' interpretations of the character.

In view of the rich history of thought about its nature, we rightly regard the term "sacramental character" as highly symbolic: it signifies many diverse enduring consequences of the sacraments of baptism, confirmation and holy orders. To define it in a particular way, then, is not necessarily to exclude other definitions of it. Our relating it here to one's place in the Church as institution does not invalidate, for example, the Church Fathers' idea of it as a metaphor for the irrevocableness of God's love or St. Thomas Aquinas' widely accepted idea of it as a participation in the priesthood of Christ (*Summa theologiae,* III, q. 63).

Recently theologians have returned to a more Augustinian view of the character. They interpret it as something more immediately perceptible than a purely interior effect in the soul, without denying that it affects a person in the depth of his being, in his soul. Thus Karl Rahner (*The Church and the Sacraments,* Herder and Herder, p. 88-90) conceives the character as the sociohistorical fact of the Church's conferral of the sacrament and one's reception of it. Eliseo Ruffini ("Character as a Concrete Visible Element of the Sacrament in Relation to the Church," *Concilium* 31, pp. 101-14) sees the characters as giving hierarchical structure to the Church in its activity of worshiping and sanctifying.

Along the same lines we may say that the sacramental character refers to the position which the baptized, confirmed or ordained person obtains in the institutional Church as a consequence of the Church's conferral of the sacrament and the individual's reception of it. Since that Church is the Body of Christ whereby he continues to exercise among men his priestly, prophetic and kingly ministries, to obtain a particular place in the institutional Church is to obtain a particular participation in Christ's royal and prophetic priesthood. The exact nature of this sharing is to be defined in terms of one's relationship to, or position in, the Church as institution.

One's place in the institutional Church has the sacramental character's quality of a sign, for one's place as publicly acknowledged is evident to everyone and points to where one stands in the Body of Christ and what one's role is in that Body. One's place in the institutional Church has the quality of being "indelible," for one's recognized place in the Church endures even if one does not continue the way of life which it calls for. It is aptly described as a spiritual reality imprinted on the soul, for one has a place in the Church, not simply as a bodily or a psychic being interacting with things, but precisely as a spiritual being, that is, as in communion with other men and women and as transcending self in the direction of God by faith in Jesus Christ.

"Full ecclesial recognition of adulthood in the Spirit," "a place in the institutional Church as a publicly acknowledged adult in the Spirit" and "the sacramental character of confirmation" are three ways of referring to the secondary special effect of confirmation. This effect endures even if one ceases to live by the Spirit; and it is a reason, along with the irrevocableness of God's gift of the Spirit's fullness, why the sacrament is not repeated in one's lifetime.

The Minister of Confirmation

Since confirmation is the Christian community's institutional acknowledgement of its baptized members' adulthood in the Spirit, an appropriate minister of the sacrament is the bishop. He has been charged with primary public responsibility for the welfare of the local Church. He symbolizes Christ the head to the members of Christ's Body; and he represents the members in their actions, in union with Christ, toward the candidate for confirmation. The bishop also shares in the primary

143

public responsibility for the universal Church because of his membership in the college of bishops with its head, the pope. Thus the conferral of confirmation by the bishop celebrates the confirmed person's relation as an adult in the Spirit to the local Church and the universal Church and to the Church's life and mission.

The new rite of confirmation refers to the bishop as the "original" minister, not the "ordinary" minister of the sacrament (RC, n. 7). This terminology expresses the idea that confirmation derives ultimately from the bishops' predecessors in the office of primary public responsibility for the welfare of the Church, namely, the Apostles. The Apostles experienced the fullness of the Spirit on Pentecost, began then boldly to bear witness to Christ and also bestowed the Spirit in a special way by the imposition of hands, at least on two occasions (Acts 8:17; 19:6). This imposition of hands very likely was not the sacrament of confirmation in the strict sense, but it was a kind of precedent or model for later developments. The term "original minister" also reflects the idea that the priest can confer confirmation on the basis of his ordination; he is not merely a delegated minister. The exercise of this ministry, however, is conditioned by the regulations of the Christian community. In the Western Church, confirmation is usually conferred by the bishop and thus more clearly celebrates the confirmed persons' relation to the local and universal Church.

The new rite of confirmation, however, provides liberally for priests in various positions and circumstances to confer the sacrament. They may do so, of course, for someone in danger of death. But two provisions are especially noteworthy. First, priests who lawfully baptize an adult, or child old enough for instruction, may confirm them, in accord with the intimate bond between baptism and confirmation and their nature as initiation to the eucharist. Priests may also confirm a validly baptized adult whom they admit to full communion in the Church (RC, n. 7b). Secondly, the bishop, or anyone who has the right by law to confer the sacrament, may associate other priests with him in conferring it. These other priests may be those holding particular offices in the diocese, the pastor of the place where confirmation is conferred, the pastors of the places to which the candidates belong or priests who have taken a special part in the candidates' preparation for the sacrament (RC, n. 8).

When priests confer confirmation, they anoint with chrism consecrated by the bishop in the Mass which is celebrated on Holy Thursday. Moreover, in the homily they should explain that the bishop is the original minister of the sacrament and why they, priests, are now ministering it (RC, n. 8). When priests are associate ministers with the bishop, the rite provides that the bishop hand to each of them the vessel of chrism with which they will anoint the candidates (RC, n. 28). Thus, even when priests confer confirmation, its relation to the bishop and hence to the whole Church, both local and universal, is indicated.

Now that we have an idea of what confirmation celebrates and what its special effects are, we can consider how it may fit into the ongoing life of the Christian community and its members.

Chapter Seven

Pastoral Considerations

On many occasions in the past year I have mentioned to people in conversation that I was writing a book on the sacrament of confirmation. With few exceptions the response was a question about what age I proposed for confirmation. That question is apparently the paramount one in people's minds. The prevalent idea appears to be that, if the right age for confirmation could be determined, the most vexing theological and pastoral problems of the sacrament would be resolved. But concern over the age for confirmation distracts from more important questions, namely, the true nature of the sacrament, catechesis for it and its value for the Christian community and its members. We have already attended to the nature of confirmation. In this chapter, therefore, after a few necessary observations about the age for confirmation, we will consider catechesis for it and some undervalued uses of it.

Possible Ages for Confirmation

At a meeting of the National Conference of Catholic Bishops in Atlanta, Georgia, in April of 1972, the Committee on Pastoral Research and Practices presented five possible ages for the sacrament of confirmation. (1) Early childhood before the first reception of the eucharist. Confirmation is thus envisioned as completing the baptismal rite and introducing a person to the eucharist. (2) About sixth grade, around the age of 11. About this age the first formal instruction in the Christian mystery is completed and a transition is begun between childhood and adolescence. (3) During adolescence, in second or third year of high school, about the age of 15 or 16. At this age a young person begins to adopt personal views and values for life. (4) At the entrance to adulthood, about the age of 21. Then a person begins to enter into the more or less definitive orientation of his life. (5) During adulthood, when a person is capable of a quite mature decision about the direction which he wishes to give to his life.

The doctrinal and pastoral pros and cons for each of these ages was considered by the committee. But the wide variety of situations in the country prompted the committee to recommend that the general norm repeated in the new rite (RC, n. 11) be adopted without modification for the country as a whole. According to that norm, in the Latin Church children receive confirmation about the age of seven: individual bishops, however, can defer confirmation to a later age in accord with the leeway given in the new rite (RC, n. 11). This recommendation was adopted by the National Conference of Catholic Bishops (*Newsletter* of the Bishops' Committee on the Liturgy, May-June, 1972).

Age and Theology

In the light of the explanation of confirmation proposed in the preceding chapters, confirmation makes sense theologically at any of the ages noted by the Committee on Pastoral Research and Practice. We speak about confirmation "making sense" theologically at any age. We are claiming that a good theological explanation of the sacrament can be given at whatever age its recipients happen to be. Religious educators need not wring their hands in despair because the theology of confirmation requires that it be conferred, let us say, on adults, while they must prepare children. The theology of the sacrament is not tied to a particular age for its recipients.

In support of this claim we note that, at whatever age confirmation is conferred, it celebrates the Holy Spirit's fullness in us. We have this fullness of the Spirit by virtue of baptism. It is, moreover, God's gift, not our achievement. The proximate primary special effect of the celebration of the Spirit's fullness in us is a special strength consisting in increased consciousness of the fullness of Christian life made possible by the Spirit within, greater attraction to that fullness of life and a sense of the community's support in pursuit of it. Theologically it is unimportant whether confirmation has this effect immediately by the celebration of the sacrament alone or mediately with the aid of post-confirmational catechesis which extends the sacrament into subsequent life. The ultimate primary special effect is holiness involving a deep life of prayer, notable love and witness individually and by participation in the life and mission of the Christian community. This effect, even in the case of adult confirmation, ordinarily emerges only gradually in the course of time through the mediation of many different experiences in life.

Infant baptism makes sense theologically, even

though the conscious Christian life issues from the sacrament only subsequently with the help of parents, community, and various experiences (see Christopher Kiesling, "Infant Baptism," *Worship* 42 [1968]:617-26). In a similar way confirmation conferred at an early age is theologically justifiable.

The secondary special effect of confirmation is full ecclesial recognition of adulthood in the Spirit. Theologically the community can give this recognition at a very early age because adulthood in the Spirit is radically present at least from the moment of baptism. Baptism is the first celebration of the gift of the Spirit although it does not celebrate that gift as emphatically as confirmation does.

On the part of baptized persons, it is relatively unimportant theologically whether they accept and begin to act upon their radical adulthood in the Spirit at the time of the community's public act acknowledging it or afterwards through the mediation of catechesis. Most important is that in the course of life — in, after or even before confirmation — they live an ever increasingly mature Christian life.

Moreover, at whatever age confirmation is conferred in recognition of adulthood in the Spirit, the rite is an empty gesture on the part of the Christian community if it does not follow up that recognition by engaging in an adult manner the confirmed person in the community's life and mission. It is theologically insignificant whether the community engages the person in an adult manner on the very day on which it confers confirmation or gradually over the years following the sacrament. Besides, we would expect the community, even in the case of adult confirmation, to increase its reliance on the confirmed person over the years after his or her confirmation. Confirmation as full ecclesial recognition of adulthood in the Spirit makes sense theologically as long as it is followed through. The community must introduce the confirmed person into the life and mission of the Church in accord with the individual's capacity until he or she is finally participating in that life and mission in a way which is adult from every point of view.

Age and Pastoral Strategy

But does confirmation at any age make sense pastorally? The theology of confirmation offered here does not answer that question. The answer is one of pastoral strategy, which requires that we stand back and survey the whole range of individual and ecclesial Christian life. We should note its diverse needs throughout its course in the field of today's world. Consideration should then be given to all the resources available to promote that life: the word of God, the seven sacraments, prayer, catechesis, retreats, religious communities and many other things. Finally, those resources should be deployed throughout the course of life in a sequence and in relationships which will most efficiently advance Christian life in individuals and the community.

Probably different deployments of the means of Christian life will be most effective in various places. Perhaps in some areas the ancient order of baptism, confirmation and eucharist at an early age, followed by an extended catechesis, will be most effective. In other places confirmation late in life will be most efficient. In the same place different arrangements of the means of Christian life will work best at different times. Hence, the question of the right age for confirmation will be answered only by research into the concrete conditions of Christian life in various places at various times and by experimentation with the age which such research suggests. Any answer which such research and experimentation yield, however, will be valid only as long as the conditions of Christian life remain stable. Any answer, therefore, will be conditional, not absolute.

In devising pastoral strategy in our country today, some factors are worth noting in regard to the age for confirmation. The first factor is a deeply-rooted practice of infant baptism and early first eucharist. This practice is supported by a detailed theology (whatever its merits) covering every angle of the practice and deeply embedded in the Catholic mind. The sacraments of initiation, in contrast to the other sacraments, celebrate Christian life in all circumstances, not only in special situations. In view of widespread infant baptism and early first eucharist, pastoral strategy may decide that at least one of the sacraments of initiation should be conferred when a person has maturity at least approaching psychological and sociological adulthood. For the over-all promotion of Christian life, it may be pastorally most effective to delay confirmation, even for a considerable period. This postponement breaks up the sacraments of initiation understood ritually. But as we noted in Chapter 2, "sacrament of initiation" may be understood theologically, that is, as concerned with the basics of life in the Spirit at all times. For the long-run good of Christian life, the ritual ideal may have to be sacrificed, except in cases of adult converts.

Another factor to consider in devising pastoral strategy is the length of time required to change deeply ingrained practices and the theologies legitimatizing them, such as those of infant baptism and early first eucharist. Decades would be required to change these practices and their theologies. It may be proposed that the ancient order of baptism, confirmation and eucharist should be maintained; the whole complex should be moved back in life to an age of greater maturity; and a rite of dedication should replace infant baptism. But this proposal is not a practical alternative for pastoral strategy concerned with the immediate future. Such a proposal might be a distant objective; but at the conference table of pastoral strategists concerned with the coming year, it is unrealistic.

Still another factor to be kept in mind is the danger of elitism or sectarianism. Christians who take their faith very seriously tend to want, and not merely expect, every Christian to have the same attitude. But Catholicism has characteristically been a religion of the masses. It welcomes into its organizational structure all men and women in the hope that they will grow into the attitudes which that structure serves and symbolizes. It tolerates a great deal of foreign and even false religiosity in individuals. It expects that in the course of time, through the Holy Spirit's influence in the resources of the Christian community, the foreign and false will be exorcised or at least counteracted. The proposal to postpone confirmation and even baptism until people demonstrate some degree of mature commitment to Christ must be watched lest it lead to an elitist Church or sect.

A second danger accompanying insistence on a mature Christian commitment as a requisite for confirmation is that of making confirmation a reward for commitment to Christ. The Church has struggled in this century to overcome the idea that reception of the eucharist is a reward for virtuous living. So that confirmation does not now become the reward for virtuous living, care must be taken in any pastoral strategy which delays confirmation until a psychologically and sociologically more mature age.

Another factor to guard against in planning pastoral strategy is exploiting the fact that children in grade school are relatively easy "to get at," while high school students and young people beyond that age are difficult to reach. The temptation exists to give grade school children the "dose of grace" which confirmation provides *ex opere operato*. If preceded and followed by a well developed catechesis, confirmation of grade school children could be pastorally effective and sensible. But the pastoral soundness of confirmation for grade school children is not based on the idea that confirmation must be given at any cost to every Christian by any device whatsoever. It is not based on a naive understanding of the *ex opere operato* efficacy of the sacraments. It does not exploit children's lack of freedom but aims at developing it.

In this discussion of the appropriate age for confirmation, we have frequently mentioned catechesis, not only before confirmation but also rarely heard-of post-confirmational catechesis. Pastoral strategy arranges the multiple resources for Christian life in a sequence and in relationships that most effectively promote Christian life in the long run. A pastoral decision on an age for confirmation must be made with an eye on catechesis for the sacrament. So we must give some consideration to that subject.

Importance of Catechesis

Preparation for confirmation has a dignity and importance that perhaps we frequently overlook. We do

not see catechesis' deep connection with the sacrament. In an emergency the Christian community's celebration of the fullness of the Spirit in one of its members can be a very simple act. One prayer is said calling upon the Father to send his Spirit upon the candidate and to give him or her the Spirit's seven gifts. Then the candidate is anointed by the minister as he says: "Receive the seal of the Holy spirit, the Gift of the Father" (RC, nn. 54-55). Normally, however, the celebration is more elaborate. It spells out at greater length in more prayers, in a homily, in the symbolic personage of the bishop, in ceremonies and in hymns the mystery celebrated.

Catechesis for confirmation also articulates in words and actions the mystery celebrated in the sacrament either about to be conferred or already conferred. So catechesis is a kind of extension of confirmation into life before and after the sacrament's reception. It is a kind of informal, nonceremonial celebration of the Spirit's fullness in us and the possibility of the fullness of the Christian life. Through the words and actions of the Christian community's catechesis for confirmation, God displays his gracious love giving his Spirit's fullness to the candidate, and so he draws the candidate ever closer to himself. In terms of classical theology, catechesis before confirmation is a bearer of actual grace disposing the recipient for the sacrament; catechesis afterwards is a bearer of actual grace activating the gifts received in the sacrament. Thus catechesis is the link which unites confirmation with daily Christian life before and after the sacrament.

Confirmational catechesis is thus a significant thread in the tapestry of life in the Spirit for both community and individual. It is part of the Christian community's life in the Spirit because by it the community serves God as he continues to communicate the fullness of his Spirit to others. Catechesis is part of life in the Spirit for Christians because by it they are more extensively and intensively assimilating the Spirit's influence into their lives.

Content: The Whole of Christian Life

The content of catechesis for confirmation obviously should be an accurate explanation of what the sacrament celebrates and what effects it is meant to have in a person's life. In pursuit of this accuracy the following suggestions are offered.

Catechesis for confirmation can well afford to begin, not with confirmation, but with Christian life as a whole. That life should be portrayed as embracing all that is truly human, calling forth the best in human nature and enabling men and women to transcend themselves in love for neighbor and for God, indeed to transcend themselves beyond what eye has seen, what ear has heard or what has dawned on man that God has prepared for those who love him (cf. I Cor. 2:9). Christian life should be presented not as a series of practices, a quantified whole, but a flowing, absorbing, whirling, flooding stream. The interaction of its various components, aspects and developments should be indicated. All this must be done much more concretely than in these sentences, of course, and the concreteness must be tailored to the intellectual and emotional capacity of those being catechized.

Several purposes are served by beginning catechesis for confirmation in this way. It appeals to everyone's interest in what to do with his or her life to make it satisfying, successful, happy. It appeals to everyone's search for values, whether they be values appropriate to children or to adults. It offsets the tendency to look at confirmation as an isolated event with little or no connection with life as a whole. If confirmation is seen as part of an attractive life, it will gain in its own attractiveness. If it is seen in relation to the whole of life, it more likely will be conceived as functioning humanly rather than mechanically or biologically. Hence, its effects will be understood not in terms of a quantity of grace, but in terms of a God-given enrichment and orientation of life. The temptation to evaluate its worth on the basis of immediately observable results will be lessened.

A second suggestion is to treat confirmation in conjunction with baptism and the eucharist. The three sacraments together fully express explicitly for Christian consciousness all the constituents of life in the Spirit generally. This expression, moreover, is overlapping. Baptism, for example, expresses to some degree the gift of the Spirit which is fully expressed in confirmation. Confirmation expresses life for the Father in Christ, a truth which baptism also expresses in its opposition to sin and death. Besides, all three sacraments concern the one life in the Spirit which is a dynamic whole, like a living organism, and not an accumulation of independent parts, like a machine. Hence, any one factor, aspect or development of Christian life or the symbolic expression of it can be adequately understood only in relation to the whole and all other components, aspects and developments.

Presenting confirmation together with baptism and the eucharist serves a particular purpose. If confirmation's celebration is seen as complementing that of baptism and the eucharist, if its special effects are seen as interacting with the effects of these other sacraments, there will be less of a tendency to regard confirmation as some kind of magic or mechanical dispenser of a quantity of grace. The impression will more easily be conveyed that confirmation is another experience in the totality of Christian life, building upon previous experiences and having consequences for those of the future. Thus confirmation will be seen as giving shape or direction to life in conjunction with other experiences.

A third suggestion for confirmational catechesis is to present confirmation in its proper relation to baptism and the eucharist. It should not be put on the same plane as those two sacraments; their priority as the major sacraments should be maintained. In particular, care should be taken not to demean baptism as celebrating the full benefits of Christ's victory over sin and death and as providing all the principles for Christian life. Special care should be taken, of course, not to attribute the gift of the Spirit simply to confirmation rather than to baptism or to attribute to confirmation more of the Spirit himself. So to attribute the gift of the Spirit to confirmation would be to treat him as a quantitative thing rather than a personal being whose influence increases in our lives as more of our personality opens to his inspiration and aid.

A fourth suggestion is to focus on what confirmation primarily celebrates, namely, the Holy Spirit's fullness in us given in baptism, making possible a full Christian life. Confirmation celebrates what God gives and does in us, not what we have or do solely on the basis of our native human endowments. Confirmation does celebrate our humanity and our achievements, but precisely as graced by God. In particular, the main emphasis should not be shifted to our Christian commitment. Confirmation does not primarily celebrate our making a commit-

159

ment, but God's gift to us of his Spirit making such a commitment possible. If we have already committed ourselves seriously to Christ before confirmation, then the sacrament celebrates, in gratitude, the gift of God which made that commitment possible and which can strengthen it in the future. If no serious commitment has been made, the sacrament celebrates, in hope, the divine Gift who makes such a commitment possible in the future.

Fifthly, the essence of confirmation should not be misrepresented by identifying it as the ratification or renewal of baptismal promises. That ratification or renewal is a predisposition for confirmation. The essence of confirmation is celebration of the Holy Spirit's fullness in us for a full Christian life as a result of baptism.

A final suggestion for the content of catechesis for confirmation is not to oversell its effects. In celebrating the Holy Spirit's fullness in us, confirmation celebrates the principle of Christian maturity, the promise of a full Christian life, the vocation to holiness. That maturity, full Christian life and holiness will actually emerge only in the course of time in the setting of opportune occasions. Then it will emerge only gradually so that what once seemed mature, full and holy will appear later as superficially so in the light of greater maturity, fullness and holiness. Even the special strength of heightened consciousness, increased attraction and sense of community support which confirmation causes may have to be mediated through post-confirmational catechesis before it is felt in a significant way, and such mediation will take time. Full ecclesial recognition of adulthood in the Spirit does not do away with the need of "job training" before one can participate fully in an adult manner in the life and mission of the Church.

Those being prepared for confirmation may be told without adequate qualifications that the sacrament will make them mature Christians, give them the fullness of Christian life, strengthen them as Christians and introduce them into adult participation in the Church's life and mission. After confirmation they discover that they are just about the same as they were before, and they do nothing other than they did before. Then they dismiss the sacrament as valueless and forget it.

But if the effects of the sacrament are not oversold, candidates will be led to understand confirmation as a promise for the future. After their confirmation the Christian community will help them to actualize the promised effects. Then the confirmed will more likely remember the sacrament as an important experience in their lives. Confirmation will continue to inspire them many years later in the pursuit of authentic Christian discipleship.

By Word and Action

The form of catechesis for confirmation should be both instruction and demonstration. Obviously candidates should be taught the theology of confirmation and its effects. Preparation should also include suggestions and directions as to how the effects of confirmation may be realized in the course of life. Therefore candidates should be instructed in what striving for the fullness of Christian life or holiness entails. They should be guided in prayer, the various kinds of prayer (vocal, mental, liturgical) and especially a deep life of prayer. The kinds of acts of self-giving love possible and appropriate in today's world should be pointed out to them. How they can witness to Christ in their individual lives and in the life and mission of the Christian community should also be explained to them. They should be informed about how Christ can be proclaimed in the modern world. Instruction on such topics coincides with the suggestion made earlier that confirmation should be presented in the context of Christian life as a whole.

Verbal instruction, however, is not enough. Equally important, perhaps more important, is demonstration of the significance of confirmation for Christian life. The confirmed should know the difference confirmation makes in Christian life by experiencing it. They may gain this experience in several ways. For example, opportunities may be given to them to discuss with patently mature Christians personal efforts to live a full Christian life in the midst of today's world. They can pray together in various ways: informally and spontaneously, silently, liturgically (celebration of the Word, eucharist, communal penance, the liturgy of the hours). They can share more fully in the life and mission of the Christian community by preparing, let us say, one of the parish's Sunday liturgies and by engaging in one of its apostolic works, for example, its care of the sick, the elderly, the poor. They can discuss the meaning of Christ for life in their school, family, neighborhood, city, nation, and be encouraged to act in one or another of these spheres to put Christian principles into action.

Demonstrations of what confirmation means in Christian life should not be artificial. A discussion of how to live Christian life in today's world will be a game if it is not with people who are earnestly intent upon such a life and are accustomed to discuss it. The opportunity to prepare a Sunday liturgy in the parish church will be a mere gimmick if parishioners do not normally do that as part of their adult Christian life in community. An apostolic project conjured up for a few weeks for the sake of confirmation candidates will demonstrate hypocrisy rather than authentic Christian life if the local community is apostolicly apathetic.

Demonstration of the meaning of confirmation should be a real apprenticeship in living a more mature Christian life. An apprenticeship implies that there are masters from whom one can learn. Demonstration or apprenticeship is the most effective way of helping recipients appreciate the value of confirmation. For such apprenticeship a Christian community vigorously living by the Spirit of Christ is necessary. For this reason, three relatively recent considerations of confirmation by highly competent scholars of liturgy and theology point out that the critical factor in confirmation is not so much the rite of confirmation or the age at which it is conferred, but genuine Spirit-filled Christian community (see Joseph Powers, "Confirmation: The Problem of Meaning," *Worship* 46 [1972]:22-29; Aidan Kavanagh, "Initiation: Baptism and Confirmation," *ibid.*, 262-76; Ralph Keifer, "Confirmation and Christian Maturity: The Deeper Issue," *ibid.*, 601-08).

Post-confirmational Catechesis

Generally catechesis before confirmation is appreciated and provided. But what emerges from our considerations is the importance of post-confirmational catechesis. This catechesis very often, if not most often, is neglected. Confirmation will be valued by those who receive it if they experience that it makes some difference in their lives. But this experience can occur only if after confirmation the Christian community helps them to live differently by enabling them to realize in their lives the effects attributed to the sacrament. In confirmation the Christian community celebrates its passing on to its members the fullness of the Spirit for a full Christian life, and it recognizes them as radically adult in the Spirit. The Christian community "lets down" the recipients if, after their confirmation, it abandons them to their previous way of life, rather than helping them to live in accord with its celebration. If the *ex opere operato* efficacy of confirmation does not do away with the need to dispose recipients before the sacrament, it also does not do away with the need to help them afterwards. Both catechetical instruction and especially demonstration after confirmation are extremely important. In fact, they are more important than pre-confirmational catechesis, as important as that is.

Catechesis for the Community

The effectiveness of confirmation is not restricted to the candidates for the sacrament, but extends also to the whole community assembled for its celebration. Confirmation celebrates the fullness of the Spirit and the promise of the fullness of Christian life in all the community's members, even in those for whom the sacrament has already been celebrated. From the celebration of confirmation for others, all those present experience heightened awareness of the fullness of the Spirit, attraction to the fullness of Christian life and a sense of the community's support in pursuit of that goal. Hence confirmation is an act which the community performs not only for the benefit of those not yet confirmed. It performs the act also for the benefit of all its members, singly and collectively.

But if confirmation is going to profit the whole

Christian community, the community needs preparatory catechesis as well as the individual whose need is the occasion for the sacrament. The community can benefit also from post-confirmational catechesis. Therefore catechesis for confirmation should be provided for the whole Christian community, that is, the whole parish or several parishes.

Such a catechesis can be accomplished through homilies at Sunday Mass in the weeks preceding confirmation. The community can be prepared also by several meetings of discussion groups in homes throughout the parish. Parents and families can be engaged in the preparation of those about to receive the sacrament. As a follow-up of confirmation, the parish may undertake some genuinely needed but short-term apostolic projects. The newly confirmed can be associated in responsible ways in these projects. Those confirmed long ago will renew their life in the fullness of the Spirit by these apostolic projects. The newly confirmed will be provided with an apprenticeship under more adult Christians; they will be able to experience that confirmation does make a difference in their lives.

Confirmation for the Community

Our pastoral considerations have covered the age for confirmation and catechesis for it. The final pastoral considerations concern some undervalued uses of confirmation. The first of these underrated uses is confirmation for the good of the Christian community and not just for the good of individuals who have not been confirmed. We have just noted in our consideration of catechesis that confirmation has an impact on the community. The value of this impact comes to light with the question of

how often confirmation should be conferred.

The answer is frequently thought of in terms of individuals not yet confirmed. Most people assume that confirmation should be received by every baptized person even though the sacrament is not absolutely necessary for salvation. Periodically a number of baptized but unconfirmed persons accumulate in a parish. Justification then exists for the bishop's coming and the people's undertaking the work involved in preparing for and performing the sacrament. In practice confirmation tends to be celebrated every two or three years. In an exceptional parish, for example, in a neighborhood of office buildings and high-rise apartments, there may be relatively few children. Confirmation may rarely be celebrated in the parish, the children being confirmed in a nearby parish more normal in its population. If confirmation were to be delayed to later in life and left to the initiative of people to seek it, several years may lapse before a large enough group emerged in a parish to justify confirmation. Perhaps individuals would be assembled from parishes throughout the diocese and confirmed in the cathedral.

Whatever may be said for or against any of these practices, the question at hand is the pastoral soundness of allowing any parish to go a long time without having confirmation, not for the sake of baptized but unconfirmed members, but for the sake of the community itself, considered as a whole and in its individual members, both confirmed and unconfirmed. It can be argued that confirmation should be celebrated in every parish at not too great intervals of time and that the need of the community for the sacrament is as significant a motive for its celebration as is an accumulation of unconfirmed members of the particular congregation.

The sacraments are the Christian community's paradigmatic celebrations of the life in the Spirit of its members singly and collectively. By these celebrations the whole people of God renew and deepen their life in the Spirit as well as pass that life on to others. The eucharist is the common means which the Christian community employs regularly and frequently to nourish life in the Spirit. But the eucharist is limited in its explicit expression of the factors, aspects and developments entailed in that life. Thus it is limited in its power to heighten consciousness of them and intensify attraction to them. It does not emphatically explicate, for example, the gift of the Spirit's fullness for a life of holiness, although it alludes to it. The main emphasis of the eucharist lies elsewhere. The full, explicit celebration of all the basic components, aspects and developments entailed in Christian life generally is found in the sacraments of initiation: baptism, confirmation and the eucharist. In order to keep the whole parish alert and alive to the whole of Christian life, all three sacraments should be celebrated in a parish with a degree of frequency compatible with the nature of each.

The need for alerting the whole community to the whole of Christian life is manifested in the general lack of consciousness of the Holy Spirit and his role in Christian life among vast numbers of Roman Catholics. Awareness of the Holy Spirit in the piety and theology of the Orthodox Church far surpasses that of the Churches of the Western world. One important means of remedying this deficiency is more widespread and frequent celebration of confirmation. This sacrament is designed precisely to celebrate and thus call the Christian people's attention to Christian life as issuing from the fullness of the Spirit within them.

In recent years many people have witnessed baptisms according to the new rite. They have remarked that they were greatly moved and realized more fully, if not almost for the first time, the significance of their own baptism. In other words the celebration of baptism has a genuine impact in the lives of all those who participate in it. Its impact is not restricted only to the lives of the individuals baptized. The celebration of confirmation has a similar extensive influence.

Progress has been made in recent years in overcoming the idea that the sacraments are celebrations of the minister, or of the minister and the so-called recipients, while the people present are merely observers and witnesses. Wider now is the recognition that the agent of sacramental celebrations is, under Christ, the whole community with the presiding minister, the recipients, and the faithful each playing a role contributing to the whole. Also increased is awareness that, through the benefits received by the so-called recipients of the sacraments, the whole community is built up in Christ. But still overlooked is the influence which the celebration of the sacraments has directly in the lives of all those present, if they are disposed. The direct communitarian effect of the sacraments has not been sufficiently recognized. This direct communitarian effect, it may be noted, is also *ex opere operato,* for it derives from the word of God mediated by the sacramental celebration, not from personal piety, which is only a disposition.

Hence, determination of how often confirmation should be celebrated in a parish depends not only on a sufficient number of unconfirmed members in its midst.

It depends also upon the need of the community to re-
fresh its consciousness that the distinctive life of its members singly and collectively springs from the fullness of
the indwelling Spirit inspiring and guiding them to a
fullness of Christian life. If some considerable period of
time has lapsed since confirmation was last had in a
parish, the sacrament should be celebrated even though
there is only one unconfirmed candidate in the community.

When Death Is Near

We may be inclined to disdain the practice of confirming those who have not been confirmed, have not
thought about it or prepared for it, but now are in
danger of death. The practice seems to reflect a crude
theology which envisions the sacraments as injections of
various kinds and quantities of grace into the soul. This
theology favors the injection into each soul of as many of
these different kinds of grace as are compatible with one
another. It urges also the injection of the maximum
quantity of grace, consistent with regulations about the
number of times a sacrament may be received. According
to this theology an unconfirmed person in danger of
death, therefore, should receive confirmation as well as
penance, anointing of the sick (if the danger is from
illness or old age) and the eucharist.

But another theology may underlie confirmation in
the danger of death. Confirmation celebrates life in the
Spirit and specifically the Spirit's fullness in us making
an abundance of that life possible. Such a celebration
would be encouraging to someone who is facing the
threat of death. Heightened consciousness of the infinitely powerful and wise Spirit within him would strengthen
his hope in a time of crisis and help him to face suffering

171

and death in a Christlike spirit. The other sacraments usually bestowed on those in danger of death heighten awareness of the other factors, aspects and developments of life in the Spirit; their celebrations and that of confirmation complement one another in making the threatened person conscious of the full range of God's favor toward him in Christ.

If the person threatened with death is an infant child or an unconscious adult, we may have some reservations about confirming this person. But even in these cases confirmation can make some sense. Confirmation celebrates life in the Spirit as flowing from his fullness within us. Life in the Spirit permeates but also transcends human life. We simply do not know what the Spirit in his fullness does within the depths of our being, for our minds cannot comprehend either the Spirit or the depths of our own being, even though we know they exist. We also know that whatever the Spirit does, *he* does it, not we. The development of our natural faculties of knowing and loving, our consciousness, our alertness, our dispositions are never the primary and essential source of life in the Spirit. At best they are the conditions within which the Spirit works what he wills; and if he wills, he can change our lives at depths and in ways we cannot comprehend. He can even change our dispositions.

In celebrating confirmation for a person, the Christian community implictly and explicitly prays that the Spirit will work within him. The community also affirms in hope that the Spirit does indeed work. Confirmation for the infant or child or unconscious adult is not magic or celestial mechanics, but the expression of the Christian community's prayer and hope for one of its members. This prayer and hope, issuing from faith in the risen Lord and offered in his name, are not in vain. We may be unable to perceive what the infinite Spirit accomplishes in the depths of a person in response to the community's prayer and hope. But our inability to perceive in no way means that confirmation is not beneficial to the person.

This reference to the mysteriousness of what the Spirit does within us recalls a conclusion which we drew at the beginning of our study. In the first chapter we noted that the many different and sometimes conflicting interpretations of confirmation remind us that the sacrament is ultimately part of "that mystery hidden from ages and generations past but now revealed to [God's] holy ones . . . the mystery of Christ in you, your hope of glory" (Col. 1:26-28). Our many words about confirmation have not removed, and could not remove, all the puzzles which the sacrament presents to our minds. But hopefully confirmation now makes some sense.

Questions for Discussion

Chapter One: A Puzzling Sacrament

1. If you have been confirmed, how would you express your understanding of confirmation at the time you received it? How would you express it today? If your idea has changed, why has it changed?

2. If you were confirmed, did the sacrament make any difference in your life? How would you describe that difference? If it did not make any difference, why do you think that is so? In view of your own experience, what suggestions would you make for the preparation of people for confirmation?

3. If you have not been confirmed, what do you expect from confirmation? Do you foresee that the sacrament will make any difference in your life? How would you describe that expected difference?

4. Of the various theories about confirmation presented in this chapter, which has appealed the most to you in the past? Which one appeals most to you now? How would you respond to the deficiencies which are pointed out in each of these theories?

5. What is your idea of human life and Christian life? Do you regard human life and Christian life as adventures into mystery, into the known unknown? How do you envision the relationship between human life and Christian life? How do you see confirmation fitting into your view?

Chapter Two: A Sacrament of Initiation

1. What has been your understanding of celebration? Did you ever think of life as made up of many different kinds of celebration? Can you give examples, other than those in the text, of many different kinds of celebration?

2. Does it make sense to celebrate the gift of the Spirit for Christian life? Why? Why does the Christian community and not only individuals celebrate the gift of the Spirit? Why is the Christian community the sign and instrument of the gift of the Spirit? What is the purpose of the Christian community's celebration of the gift of the Spirit for its members?

3. Have you ever before thought of baptism and confirmation as celebrations of the gift of the Spirit for Christian life? Does the idea of the sacraments as celebrations of life in the Spirit help you to understand better and appreciate more what the sacraments are and what they do? How does this idea help you? Why are the preaching of the Word and the seven sacraments called paradigms or models of the Church's many celebrations of life in the Spirit?

4. How did Christ provide for the celebration of the gift of the Spirit? Can you describe the historical development of the sacrament of confirmation? How would

you explain Christ's institution of confirmation? Are the ideas expressed in this chapter about the development and institution of confirmation different from the ideas you have had? How do the ideas which you have differ from the ideas presented here?

5. Have you previously heard confirmation called a sacrament of initiation? What did that mean to you? How would you state the interpretation given to "sacrament of initiation" in this chapter? How are the sacraments of initiation distinguished from the other sacraments?

Chapter Three: The Holy Spirit's Fullness in Us

1. Can you point to some moments in your life when you said to yourself, "If only I had known!"? Have you ever said this in connection with your Christian life? How would you describe your experience? What do you think your fellow Christians in the Christian community could have done to prevent you from having had to say that? What could you have done?

2. What is your idea of the Holy Spirit? How did you arrive at that idea? How do you see the Holy Spirit fitting into your life? What experiences in your life do you see especially as the result of the Holy Spirit's influence in you? Why do you regard these experiences as the work of the Holy Spirit?

3. What evidence is there from Scripture that baptism celebrates the gift of the Holy Spirit? For this fact, can you give evidence from Scripture which is not included in this chapter? What evidence is there from the rite

of baptism that it celebrates the gift of the Holy Spirit? Can you produce additional evidence from the rite of baptism?

4. What are the different meanings that can be given to the phrase "the Holy Spirit's fullness"? What reasons are given in this chapter for saying that confirmation celebrates the Holy Spirit's fullness *in us*? How would you explain this idea to someone? How does the rite of confirmation indicate that it celebrates the Holy Spirit's fullness in us?

5. Can you give an example of one thing or event which is celebrated in two or more different ways in order to bring out its different aspects? Can you explain how both baptism and confirmation are celebrations of the gift of the Holy Spirit and yet two different sacraments? What do we mean when we say that confirmation "complements" or "completes" or "perfects" baptism?

Chapter Four: Growth in the Life of the Spirit

1. Reflecting on some recent celebration in which you shared, can you describe how that celebration influenced you? What was your mood when you began celebrating? What was your mood during and after it? Did you become more aware or appreciative of some thing or event as a result of the celebration? Did the celebration make any difference in your life, either for a time or permanently? Did the celebration have any impact on you which you noticed only some time after the celebration was over? If the celebration had no effect on you, can you

determine why this was so?

2. What is the purpose of the symbolic words, actions, things, images, and personages which make up the sacraments? How would you explain the idea that through the preached word of God and the sacraments we come into contact with Jesus Christ? How have you understood the statement that the sacraments confer God's grace? At what points does the understanding you have had of this statement agree with, and differ from, the understanding presented in this chapter? If God's grace comes to us in many ways through various activities in which we engage, why are there sacraments?

3. How would you answer someone who claims that the sacraments do not have any noticeable effect in people's lives and are, therefore, a waste of time? If the sacraments fail to influence our lives, is this due to some deficiency in the sacraments or in us? What would some of these deficiencies be?

4. How should we understand the statement that a common effect of the sacraments is the increase, strengthening, perfecting, expanding and intensification of God's grace in us or of Christian life? Have you experienced this growth at any time? How would you describe your experience? Did you experience it with your own confirmation?

5. Why is the primary special effect of confirmation designated as the fullness of Christian life? What connection do you see between saying confirmation celebrates the Holy Spirit's fullness in us and saying confirmation's effect is the fullness of Christian life? Why is the fullness of Christian life attributed to confirmation rather than to some other sacrament? How would you distinguish from one another the three sacraments of initiation, namely,

179

Chapter Five: The Fullness of Christian Life

1. What images come to your mind when you hear the words "holiness," "mystical life," "contemplation"? How do your images match the ideas presented in this chapter about these things? Are you acquainted with any people who appear to you to live a full Christian life, or at least show signs of advancing toward it? How would you describe their life? Where do you stand in pursuit of a full Christian life?

2. What is the special strength which confirmation gives? Do you think a person has to be explicitly conscious of this special strength to have it? How would you explain the connection between the special strength which confirmation gives and the fullness of Christian life which is attributed to confirmation as its ultimate effect? Can you give some examples of obligations which arise from within us and are not merely externally imposed, as is the obligation of the confirmed to spread and defend the faith? What experiences in your life have given you special strength similar to that which is attributed to confirmation?

3. How would you describe Christian maturity? How would you describe your own development toward Christian maturity? What experiences have been most significant for your growth as a Christian? Would you count confirmation among these? Why or why not? If not, can you still see any way in which your confirmation has influenced you?

4. How would you explain to someone what "baptism of the Spirit" is? How is it related to the sacraments of baptism and confirmation? Do you know anyone who has experienced baptism of the Spirit, whether or not that name is used for the experience? Have you experienced any significant changes or conversions in the course of your life? Do you think any of them, or several of them together, was baptism in the Spirit, or do you think they were lesser conversions advancing you toward baptism in the Spirit? What is your reaction to speaking in tongues and such unusual phenomena? Have you ever witnessed these forms of prayer and praise? What value do you attach to them?

5. What do you understand by "Christian commitment"? How does your understanding fit with the meanings given to the words in this chapter? Have you experienced different degrees of Christian commitment in the course of your life? Can you see any connection between your confirmation and your commitment to Christ at any time? Do you think that it makes sense to describe confirmation as the sacrament of commitment?

Chapter Six: Full Ecclesial Recognition of Adulthood in the Spirit

1. Can you identify some factors in the life of your family which pertain to your family as a community of people sharing common beliefs and values? Can you identify certain patterns of interaction among the members of your family, that is, institutionalized interactions? Can you make similar identifications in the activities of the people who make up your school or world of

work? Can you give examples, beyond those mentioned in chapter six, of activities which pertain to the Church as community and to the Church as institution?

2. Have you ever experienced a growth in unity with the Church as a community of people sharing common beliefs and values? How would you describe this experience? What led to it? What followed from it? Have the sacraments ever led you to it or expressed it after it had occurred? Did your confirmation lead to or express greater solidarity with the Church as community? If not, why do you think it failed to do so? Do you feel any greater solidarity with or responsibility toward fellow Christians when they are confirmed? Should you? Why? How would you describe this solidarity and responsibility?

3. Could you explain how receiving a diploma in a high school graduation is an institutional recognition of a person's place in the human community? What is the relationship of a legal marriage ceremony to the love of a couple who, inspired by that love, decide to share life together? What responsibilities arise for the Church as an institution when it confirms its members? How do you think those responsibilities can be fulfilled? What responsibilities arise for the confirmed and how can they fulfill them?

4. In what sense does confirmation bestow *full* ecclesial recognition of adulthood in the Spirit? Does this recognition mean that the confirmed person will immediately act as an adult, mature, fully committed Christian? How is full ecclesial recognition of adulthood in the spirit related to one's place in the Church? What has been your idea of the sacramental character of confirmation? How is that idea similar to the idea expressed in

this chapter? How is it different?

5. Why is the bishop the original minister of the sacrament of confirmation? What does the bishop symbolize? How does this symbolism relate to confirmation? What is symbolized by several priests sharing with the bishop in conferring confirmation?

Chapter Seven: Pastoral Considerations

1. What age do you consider the most appropriate for confirmation? What are your reasons for selecting that age? Are your reasons theological, that is, based on the nature of confirmation, of the Christian life or of the Church? Or are your reasons pastoral, that is, based on the needs for effective promotion of Christian life? What would be the over-all pastoral strategy into which you would place confirmation?

2. If your idea of the appropriate age for confirmation differs from the prevalent one in your area, how would you proceed to prepare people for changing the age of confirmation? What objections could be raised to your proposal? How would you answer the objections? Are there any misunderstandings about the sacrament which might result from its conferral at the age you suggest? How would you prevent these misunderstandings?

3. How would you prepare people for confirmation at the age you think is most appropriate? What theological ideas would you emphasize? What practical demonstrations of full Christian life would you provide? How would you follow up confirmation? How would you answer these same questions for confirmation at the age accepted in your area if that age differs from the one you

personally think is best?

4. How would you describe the relationship of confirmation to the Christian community, especially the parish community? In what sense does the whole community and not only the individuals who are confirmed benefit from confirmation? Have you ever experienced a strong influence of God's word and grace on the occasion of someone else's reception of confirmation or some other sacrament? If confirmation benefits the whole community, how do you explain this? How often do you think confirmation should be celebrated in a parish? How should a parish prepare for and participate in confirmation?

5. What does death mean to people in our culture? What does it mean to you? What does it mean to one who is living a full Christian life? Why does the Christian community provide sacraments for those facing death? Why does it provide confirmation for them if they have not been confirmed? How would you describe the benefit a person facing death can derive from the sacraments, including confirmation if he has not been confirmed?

Design and photographs by Michael Reynolds.
Pictures taken at Assumption and St. Antoninus parishes, Cincinnati, with Archbishop Joseph L. Bernardin confirming.